The information contained in this book is based on the ___ research at the time of printing and is very general in nature. Readers should not rely on the general information given in this book as a substitute for professional up to date advice. The author cannot accept any responsibility for any losses, damages or adverse effects that may result from the use of information contained in this book.

First published in Australia in 2023 by KDP self-publishing

A catalogue record for this book is available from the National Library of Australia

Cover Design: Midjourney

For my family.

Jazz and Maddison

I love what I do for work, but I love who I do it for.

Table of Contents

INTRODUCTION:

The Rise of Artificial Intelligence

As a technologist I love using technology in my day-to-day life. Whether it's at work embedding new AI tools into workflows, on the go using my phone to help me navigate a foreign city, or at home getting my Google hub to set timers, video call relatives, or control appliances. I've built a career out of being a technology specialist and digital manager in the architectural, engineering, and construction industry. Recently I, like a lot of people out there, have dived headfirst into the world of artificial intelligence (AI). I've taught myself everything I know so far using a healthy dose of curiosity paired with a lot of trial and error and a lot of reading, and I do mean a lot.

This exploration has led to interviews, media publications, keynote speaker roles, panel discussions, and spending a lot of time with artificial intelligence platforms (too many to name and list here). However, I have found myself increasingly experiencing negative effects from technology overload—struggling to disconnect, anxiety from trying to keep up with new AI developments, and even simply trying to find harmony or balance in a life soaked with technology use and a reliance on a lot of these tools. To be honest I felt this anxiety-inducing overload before I ventured into the world of AI. AI itself seems to have only increased that anxiety, as the way I work is changing, how many tools I now use has increased, and simply keeping up with developments in the AI space is like trying to drink from a fire hydrant. It's these experiences in my day-to-day work and personal life, conversations with family and colleagues as well as experts across the field and in different industries, along with a large list of musings, thoughts, and notes from the last two years that led me to write this book.

This book is somewhere between a chronicle to understanding artificial intelligence, its history, and its current and future application, and a guide that details our human traits in point form and offers solutions around the urgent importance of cultivating, nurturing, and embracing them as technology continues to rapidly change the world around us and our place as humans in it.

As we stand on the brink of the fourth industrial revolution, we are not just passive spectators but active participants in an era shaped by exceptional technological advancements. These advancements are redefining our lifestyles, our work, and the very nature of our interactions. Among the cavalcade of emerging technologies, AI has recently had a huge impact. Once a speculative concept of science fiction and intellectual discourse, AI has now seamlessly blended into our lives, becoming an influential and transformative force that transcends boundaries.

In the last few decades, artificial intelligence (AI) has emerged as one of the most transformative forces. In 2022 there were numerous breakthroughs that have well and truly thrust AI back into the spotlight and seen it rapidly evolve. AI has quickly moved from a concept confined to the realms of science fiction and academia to a pervasive technology, influencing nearly every aspect of our daily lives. As AI continues to advance, it is essential to reflect on the implications of this technological revolution and explore ways to preserve our humanity in an increasingly digitised world. This book aims to provide insights, guidance, and inspiration to help readers navigate the age of artificial intelligence while cherishing their human essence.

The roots of AI date back to the mid-twentieth century, marked by a bold vision harboured by a group of forward-thinking computer scientists and mathematicians. [1] They dared to dream of machines that could replicate human cognition. This audacious idea lit the fuse for a technological expedition, traversing several milestones. The journey was propelled by leaps in computational power, the advent of innovative machine learning algorithms, and the exponential growth of data availability. Today, AI's footprints are imprinted across numerous sectors, including but not limited to healthcare, education, finance, and transportation. It has revolutionised our problem-solving techniques, decision-making processes, and interactions with technology. [2]

Yet, the swift rise of AI brings along its set of challenges and controversies. Alongside the undeniable advantages of efficiency, accuracy, and cost-effectiveness, concerns bubble up about the potential eclipse of distinct human traits and values. [3] As we assign more tasks and decisions to AI, we risk distancing ourselves from qualities that lend us our unique humanity—such as creativity, empathy, and emotional intelligence. Moreover, the burgeoning dependence on AI spurs debates around ethical dimensions, the evolving labour market, and the psychological repercussions of automation on human relationships and mental health.

To address these concerns, this book seeks to provide a well-rounded guide to flourishing in a world increasingly governed by AI. We must ensure that our march towards a technologically advanced future does not necessitate a departure from our human roots. Through a sequence of carefully designed chapters, we will investigate the importance of embracing our human uniqueness, cultivating emotional intelligence, forging deep human connections, fostering creativity and innovation, and maintaining a moral and ethical perspective in the development and deployment of AI.

By nurturing a sophisticated understanding of AI and its societal impacts, we aspire to strike a delicate balance. We aim to embrace the boons of technological advancement while preserving the fundamental essence of our humanity, a precious attribute that no machine can replicate.

We are embarking on a journey through the labyrinth of AI, with its intricate challenges and vast opportunities. Let's unite in this exploration and find strategies to preserve our authentic humanness in a world where machines are continually expanding the realms of possibility. This book is an invitation to join this journey, a shared quest for maintaining our human identity in a world irrevocably transformed by AI. It's a call to navigate the future, not with fear of obsolescence, but with the hope and conviction that our unique human attributes will continue to distinguish us, even in an age that is increasingly automated.

Together, let's envision a future where AI and humanity are not adversaries, but allies. A future where technology serves humanity, amplifying our potential, and a future where despite the automated exterior, the core remains deeply and unapologetically human. Let's remain human in the age of artificial intelligence.

The Importance of Retaining Our Humanity

As artificial intelligence continues to permeate nearly every facet of our lives, the question of what it means to be human in the age of AI becomes increasingly relevant. While AI has brought about many positive changes and advancements, it is crucial to recognise the importance of retaining our humanity. By nurturing the traits that set us apart from machines, we can continue to thrive in an AI-driven world without losing our essential human qualities. Let's briefly look at the reasons why preserving our humanity is vital and how we can achieve this goal.

Human beings are inherently imbued with an ensemble of qualities that create a stark delineation between us and artificial constructs. Our aptitude for empathy, creativity, intuition, and emotional intelligence equips us with the ability to forge connections, concoct novel ideas, and steer through intricate social scenarios. These inherent attributes not only carve out our identity but also underpin the structure of our society, shaping our cultural tapestry and shared values.

One of the core aspects of humanity lies in our ability to experience emotions and make moral judgements. [4] Moral decisions are often posed as gut-wrenching and dramatic emotional choices. While AI systems can analyse vast amounts of data and make decisions based on algorithms, they lack the emotional and moral depth that characterises human decision-making. Preserving our humanity ensures that we continue to make choices rooted in empathy, compassion, and ethical considerations, rather than purely data-driven logic.

Humans are inherently social creatures, and our ability to build connections and form communities plays a crucial role in our well-being and development. [5] We as a species have this innate drive to develop build and maintain interpersonal connections. By retaining our humanity, we can maintain meaningful relationships and foster social bonds, which are essential for mental and emotional health. These social bonds are formed so early in life, from a young age they are an essential part of the human experience and play a pivotal role in guiding our personal and emotional development. AI can augment our lives, but it cannot replace the value and importance of human connection.

Human ingenuity has driven the world's most remarkable innovations and breakthroughs. Human ingenuity is the way in which human minds have influenced how we think, work, play, construct, and conduct friendships and other relationships, interact with each other, find solutions to problems, cause problems, transform things, and rationalise thought. It also considers the consequences of human thought and action. History is full of examples of humans as thinkers, inventors, and creators from all subject areas. Human ingenuity goes beyond looking solely at individuals and looks at human contributions both in context and as part of an ongoing process, seeing them as logical, clever, and reasoning, as well as illogical, fallible, and devious. Our ability to think creatively, imagine new possibilities, and take risks is an integral part of our human identity. As we retain our humanity, we can continue to innovate, inspire, and explore new frontiers in art, science, and technology.

As AI systems become increasingly sophisticated, ethical concerns surrounding their development and deployment will continue to grow. [6] AI's game-changing promise to do things like improve efficiency, bring down costs, and accelerate research and development has been tempered of late with worries that these complex, opaque systems may do more societal harm than economic good. With virtually no government oversight at the time of writing this book, private companies use AI software to make determinations about health and medicine, employment, creditworthiness, and even criminal justice without having to answer for how they're ensuring that programs aren't encoded, consciously or unconsciously, with structural biases. By preserving our humanity, we can ensure that the pursuit of technological advancement remains grounded in human values and moral principles. This will help to create a future where AI is developed and used responsibly, minimising potential harm and maximising its benefits for society.

The endeavour to preserve our humanity doesn't entail resisting AI or denying its potential. Instead, it underscores the need for a balanced perspective that appreciates the boons of AI while concurrently cherishing our human virtues. This comprehensive understanding of our humanity will allow us to envision a future where AI and humans coexist harmoniously, playing off each other's strengths and offsetting weaknesses. Artificial intelligence is becoming good at many human jobs—diagnosing disease, translating languages, providing customer service—and it's improving what seems like daily. This is raising relevant fears that AI will replace human workers across numerous industries. But that's not the inevitable, or even most likely, outcome. Never before have digital tools been so responsive to us, nor we to our tools. While AI will radically change how work gets done and who does it, the technology's larger impact will be in complementing and augmenting human capabilities, not replacing them.

In essence, the importance of retaining our humanity in the AI era is a subject of monumental significance. By consciously nurturing our distinctive human traits and advocating a balanced perspective, we can thrive in this AI-dominated epoch without compromising our identity. In the subsequent chapters, we will delve into practical strategies and insights to fortify our humanity in various aspects of life— from fostering emotional intelligence and creativity to nurturing human connections and navigating the moral conundrums posed by AI.

[1] https://decrypt.co/resources/a-brief-history-of-artificial-intelligence-ai-from-turing-to-iot

[2] https://www.brookings.edu/research/how-artificial-intelligence-is-transforming-the-world/

[3] https://www.wired.com/story/artificial-intelligence-animals-anthropomorphism/

[4] https://www.ncbi.nlm.nih.gov/pmc/articles/PMC4934695/

[5] https://mgiep.unesco.org/article/humans-are-social-and-emotional-beings#:~:text=Humans%20are%20born%20with%20an,learning%20and%20higher%2Dorder%20cognition.

[6] https://news.harvard.edu/gazette/story/2020/10/ethical-concerns-mount-as-ai-takes-bigger-decision-making-role/

CHAPTER 1: UNDERSTANDING ARTIFICIAL INTELLIGENCE

History and Development of AI

The history and development of artificial intelligence is a story of remarkable progress, ambition, and evolving understanding of what it means for machines to think and learn. This chapter will provide an overview of the key milestones, breakthroughs, and challenges that have shaped the AI landscape as we know it today.

The concept of intelligent machines has been part of human imagination for centuries, with roots in ancient myths and legends. However, the modern foundations of AI can be traced back to the mid-twentieth century when pioneering computer scientists, mathematicians, and cognitive psychologists began to explore the possibilities of creating machines capable of replicating human thought processes. [7]

Early efforts in the AI space were hampered by two main factors: computing processes and cost. Before 1949 computers lacked a key prerequisite for intelligence: they couldn't store commands; they could only execute them. In other words, computers could be told what to do; they just couldn't remember what they had done. Secondly, computing at this time was extremely expensive. In the late '40s early '50s, the cost to lease a computer ran up to $200,000 a month. Only large universities and big technology companies could afford to explore in these very much uncharted pursuits of AI.

In 1950, British mathematician and computer scientist Alan Turing published his seminal paper, "Computing Machinery and Intelligence," which introduced the idea of the *Turing test*—a criterion for determining whether a machine can exhibit intelligent behaviour indistinguishable from that of a human. Alan Turing posed the question—"Can machines think?" His paper argues that there is no convincing argument that machines cannot think intelligently like humans, and different approaches can be undertaken in hopes of advancing machine intelligence. This paper laid the groundwork for future research in AI. [8]

The term *artificial intelligence* was coined in 1956 at the Dartmouth Conference, where a group of researchers, including conference hosts John McCarthy and Marvin Minsky, as well as Cliff Shaw and Allen Newell, came together to discuss their shared interest in machine intelligence. A proof-of-concept AI called Logic Theorist was initialised at this event. Logic theorist was a program designed to mimic the problem-solving skills of a human and was funded by Research and Development (RAND) Corporation. It's considered by many to be the first artificial intelligence program. Whilst John McCarthy had imagined the conference to be a great collaborative effort, the coming together of the top researchers from various fields and finding agreement on standard methods for the field, the conference fell short of his expectations. Despite this, everyone at the conference aligned with the sentiment that AI was achievable. Just how significant this conference was cannot be understated as it marked the beginning of AI as a formal research field and set the direction for the next twenty years of AI research. [9]

Early AI research focused on two main approaches: The first being *symbolic AI*, also known as *rule-based AI*, *classic AI*, and *good old-fashioned AI* (GOFAI), which aimed to represent human knowledge using symbols and logical rules. This approach trains artificial intelligence the same way the human brain learns. It learns to understand the world by forming internal symbolic representations of its "world". Symbols play a vital role in the human thought and reasoning process. We learn both objects and abstract concepts, then create rules for dealing with these concepts. These rules can be formalised in a way that captures everyday knowledge. Symbolic AI mimics this mechanism and attempts to explicitly represent human knowledge through human-readable symbols and rules that enable the manipulation of those symbols. Symbolic AI entails embedding human knowledge and behaviour rules into computer programs.

The second approach is *connectionist AI*, which developed out of attempts to understand how the human brain works at the neural level and, in particular, how people learn and remember. Connectionist AI gets its name from the typical network typology that most of the algorithms in this class employ. The most popular technique in this category is the *artificial neural network* (ANN). This consists of multiple layers of nodes, called *neurons*, that process input signals, combine them with some weight coefficients, and feed them to the next layer. The key aspect of connectionist AI is that the user does not specify the rules of the domain being modelled. The network "discovers" the rules from the training data. The user provides input data and sample output data, and connectionist algorithms then apply statistical regression models to adjust the weight coefficients in a direction that minimises the cumulative error from all the training data points. If enough sample data is used, these algorithms won't need a model of the world. They will statistically infer that from the data. This is a hugely powerful characteristic but also a weakness. [10]

In the 1960s and 1970s, AI researchers began developing algorithms that allowed machines to learn from data, rather than relying on predefined rules as explored in the earlier paragraph on connectionist AI. This shift marked the beginning of machine learning, a subfield of AI focused on creating algorithms capable of learning from and making predictions based on data. [11] Those predictions may include determining if a piece of fruit in a photograph is an apple or a banana at your grocery store's self-checkout scanner, or whether an item crossing the road in front of a self-driving car is, in fact, a human being. The greatest difference between this and regular computer software is that a person did not write the code that tells the system how to detect the difference between an apple and a banana. Instead, the machine learning model was taught how to consistently distinguish between the fruits by being trained on a massive volume of data, in this case a huge number of pictures identified as including a banana or an apple.

Machine learning is split into two main categories, supervised and un-supervised. *Supervised learning* essentially teaches machines by example. It is defined by its use of labelled datasets. These datasets are used to supervise algorithms as they classify data or predict outcomes accurately. Using labelled data (inputs and outputs), the model can measure its own accuracy and learn over time. Supervised machine learning is used in two main problems: classification and regression. *Classification problems* use an algorithm to accurately assign data into specific categories, such as apples and bananas. *Regression problems* use an algorithm to understand the relationship between dependant and independent variables.

The second category of machine learning is *unsupervised learning*, where algorithms analyse and cluster unlabelled data sets. They identify patterns in data, trying to spot similarities that split data into categories. These algorithms discover hidden patterns or data groupings without the need for human intervention. Unsupervised machine learning is used for three main tasks: clustering, association, and dimensionality reduction. *Clustering* is a data mining technique or grouping unlabelled data based on their similarities or differences. It is useful for market segmentation or image compression. *Association* uses different rules to find relationships between variables in a given dataset, used heavily for market basket analysis—think "customers who bought this also bought . . ." *Dimensionality reduction* is a learning technique used when the number of features in a given dataset is too high. It reduces the data inputs whilst preserving data integrity.

One of the earliest machine learning algorithms, the *perceptron*, was developed by Frank Rosenblatt in 1957/1958. [12] The perceptron is an algorithm for supervised learning of binary classifiers. A *binary classifier* is a function that can decide if an input represented as a vector of numbers belongs to a specific class. The perceptron was intended to be a machine, not a software. However, it was implemented as a custom-built piece of hardware known as the "Mark 1 perceptron". This machine was designed for image recognition. It had four hundred photocells randomly connected to neurons.

The AI winter of the 1980s and early '90s ('87 to '93 to be exact) saw a significant decline in funding for AI research, as it was widely believed that the field of AI had failed to achieve its grandiose objectives, and nowhere in the field had the discoveries made produced the impact that was promised. The field didn't disappear entirely; some important advances were made during this time, including the development of neural networks, decision trees, support vector machines, and Bayesian networks.

In the early 2000s, a new approach to machine learning called *deep learning* began to gain traction. Deep learning involves training artificial neural networks with multiple layers, allowing them to model complex patterns and representations in data. Each level learns to transform its input data into a more abstract representation. The word *deep* in deep learning refers to the number of layers through which the data is transformed. This breakthrough was made possible by advancements in computing power, as well as the availability of large, labelled datasets for training. [13]

The success of deep learning can be attributed to several key developments, including the introduction of the back propagation algorithm for training multi-layer neural networks by Geoffrey Hinton, [14] the development of convolutional neural networks (CNNs) by Yann LeCun, [15] and the rise of graphical processing units (GPUs) for accelerating neural network computations. Back propagation tests for errors working backward from output to input nodes are very useful tools for improving the accuracy of predictions in data mining and machine learning. A convolutional neural network is a deep learning algorithm that takes an input image and assigns importance in the form of weights and biases to various objects in the image to then be able to differentiate one from the other. With enough training, CNNs are able to learn these filters and characteristics. GPUs or *graphical processing units* are used in a wide range of applications and are best known for their capabilities in gaming. GPUs have become quite popular in AI, as they can dramatically accelerate additional workloads in high-performance computing, deep learning, and more.

Despite the rapid progress in AI, several challenges remain, including ensuring the ethical use of AI, addressing issues of transparency and explainability, and mitigating biases embedded in AI systems. [16] People do tend to fear AI, as the technology can be hard to explain and humans tend to fear what they do not understand. This can cause our imaginations to run wild. AI does not have to be as opaque as it may seem. AI can be transparent, which is where the distinction between white box and black box AI is important. *White box AI models* use just a few rules or parameters, generally in the form of decision trees or linear workflows, which are easily understood by humans. *Black box AI models* use hundreds or even thousands of decision trees and even billions of parameters to inform their outputs. Humans could never understand models this large.

Ethical use of AI has always been a concern for those inside and outside the field. We are currently seeing governments the world over rushing to come to terms with and develop guidelines, policies, and frameworks to ensure AI is safe, secure, and reliable. Ethical AI needs to be thought about at an individual, community, and country level. AI lacks transparency, and AI-based decisions are susceptible to inaccuracies, discriminatory outcomes, and embedded or inserted bias.

While AI has achieved impressive feats in specialised tasks, creating systems capable of general intelligence or human-like reasoning across a wide range of tasks remains an elusive goal.

As we look toward the future, AI research will likely focus on the following directions:

- General artificial intelligence: Developing AI systems that can perform multiple tasks and adapt to new situations, much like human intelligence.
- Explainable AI: Creating AI models that can provide understandable and transparent explanations for their decisions, helping to build trust and ensure ethical use.

- Human-AI collaboration: Exploring ways for humans and AI systems to work together effectively, leveraging the strengths of both to achieve optimal outcomes.
- AI ethics and policy: Establishing guidelines, regulations, and best practices for the responsible development and deployment of AI, addressing concerns related to privacy, security, and fairness.
- AI for social good: Applying AI to address pressing societal challenges such as climate change, healthcare, and education, with a focus on promoting equity and inclusion.

By addressing these challenges and embracing the potential of AI, we can continue to push the boundaries of what is possible while ensuring that the technology is developed and used in a manner that benefits all of humanity. We seem to be in the "move fast and break things" period of AI as we wrap up 2023. If the industry understands and weighs the benefits and risks, partnered with some reasonable and hopefully nonstifling regulation, we will see AI developed safely and reliably. In the next chapter, we will explore the human traits that differentiate us from AI, such as creativity, empathy, and intuition, and discuss the importance of embracing and nurturing these qualities in an increasingly automated world.

[7] https://decrypt.co/resources/a-brief-history-of-artificial-intelligence-ai-from-turing-to-iot

[8] https://medium.com/@jetnew/a-summary-of-alan-m-turings-computing-machinery-and-intelligence-fd714d187c0b

[9] https://courses.cs.washington.edu/courses/csep590/06au/projects/history-ai.pdf

[10] https://blog.re-work.co/the-difference-between-symbolic-ai-and-connectionist-ai/#:~:text=A%20system%20built%20with%20connectionist,is%20an%20artificial%20neural%20network.

[11] https://www.ibm.com/topics/machine-learning#:~:text=Machine%20learning%20is%20a%20branch,rich%20history%20with%20machine%20learning.

[12] https://www.freecodecamp.org/news/the-history-of-ai/

[13] https://en.wikipedia.org/wiki/Deep_learning#History

[14] https://towardsdatascience.com/learning-backpropagation-from-geoffrey-hinton-619027613f0

[15] https://en.wikipedia.org/wiki/Yann_LeCun

[16] https://www2.deloitte.com/content/dam/Deloitte/nl/Documents/innovatie/deloitte-nl-innovation-bringing-transparency-and-ethics-into-ai.pdf

Key Concepts and Breakthroughs

The development of artificial intelligence has been marked by numerous key concepts, techniques, and breakthroughs that have shaped the field and paved the way for modern AI systems. In this section, we will provide an overview of the foundational ideas and milestones that have played a significant role in the evolution of AI, helping to create the powerful and versatile technologies we see today.

In the early days of AI research, a primary approach was *symbolic AI*, also known as *good old-fashioned AI* (GOFAI). This approach sought to replicate human intelligence by representing knowledge using symbols and logical rules. [17] Symbols play a critical role in the human thought and reasoning process. If I tell you I saw a dog chasing a ball, you can quickly imagine an image. We learn both objects and abstract concepts, and we then create rules to deal with these concepts. Symbolic AI mimics that structure and attempts to explicitly represent human knowledge through human-readable symbols and rules that enable the manipulation of those symbols. Symbolic AI entails embedding human knowledge and behaviour rules into computer programs. Key developments in symbolic AI include the following:

- The development of Logic Theorist by Allen Newell and Herbert A. Simon in 1956. This was the first program to perform automated reasoning and has been described as one of the first AI programs. Logic Theorist created better proofs than human mathematicians and actually proved thirty-eight of fifty-two theorems in Whitehead and Russell's *Principia Mathematica*, whilst also finding new and more elegant proofs. [18]
- The creation of the General Problem Solver (GPS) by Newell, Simon, and Shaw in 1957, which aimed to solve problems using human-like reasoning. [19] GPS was intended to provide a core set of processes that could be used to solve a number of different problems. Problem solvers such as this involve means-ends analysis—that is, breaking a problem down into subcomponents and solving each of those. GPS would take a goal and divide it into smaller subgoals or tasks and attempt to solve each of those. Whilst it was intended to be a general problem solver, it ended up only being applicable to well-defined problems, such as proving theorems in word puzzles, chess, or geometry.
- The invention of the LISP programming language by John McCarthy in 1958, which became the primary language for AI research and development. LISP is the second-oldest programming language after FOTRAN and provided the first read-eval-print loop to support rapid program development. Compiled functions could be freely mixed with interpreted functions. [20]

An alternative approach to symbolic AI, *connectionism*, focused on modelling cognitive processes using artificial neural networks inspired by the human brain and its interconnected neurons. [21] *Connectionist AI* uses something called a *perceptron* to represent a single neuron. A platform built using connectionist AI gets smarter through increased exposure to data as it learns the patterns and relationships within the data. Connectionist AI is great when you have a lot of high-quality data to feed into the algorithm, and while this model will get more intelligent with continued exposure, it all starts with a solid foundation of accurate data to kick-start the training process. Key milestones in connectionism include the following:

- The development of the perceptron by Frank Rosenblatt in 1957/58, considered one of the earliest artificial neural networks. [22] By modern standards the perceptron is an extremely simple artificial neural network. However, its design still applies more broadly to neural network architecture today. The perceptron is a supervised learning binary classification algorithm that categorises input data into one of two separate states based on training carried out on prior input data.

- The invention of the backpropagation algorithm by Paul Werbos in 1974, which enabled the efficient training of multi-layer neural networks. [23] Backpropagation is an algorithm designed to test for errors working from output nodes backward to input nodes. It improves the accuracy of predictions in data mining and machine learning. They are useful in training neural networks because they efficiently compute the gradient of the loss function with respect to neural network weights. This approach gets rid of the inefficient process of directly computing the gradient against each individual weight.

- The creation of Hopfield networks by John Hopfield in 1982, which introduced the concept of *recurrent neural networks* (RNNs) and demonstrated their ability to store memories. [24] John Hopfield introduced recurrent artificial neural networks in his paper titled: "Neural Networks and Physical Systems with Emergent Collective Computational Abilities." Hopfield networks are capable of producing emergent associative memory, which is a system in which memory recall is initiated by the associability of an input pattern to a memorised one. Simply put, associative memory allows for the retrieval and completion of memory using only an incomplete or noisy portion of it.

Machine learning (ML), a subfield of AI focused on developing algorithms that can learn from and make predictions based on data, has been instrumental in the advancement of AI. This field is devoted to understanding and developing methods that allow machines to "learn" methods that leverage data to improve computer performance on a range of tasks. ML algorithms build a model based on sample data, which is referred to as *training data* to make predictions and decisions without being specifically programmed to do so. ML is widely used today in a number of ways, including speech recognition, email filtering, banking software to detect unusual transactions, and making personal recommendations on platforms such as Netflix and Spotify. Key developments in machine learning include the following:

- The introduction of decision trees in the 1980s, which provided a simple and interpretable method for classification and regression tasks. [25] *Decision tree learning* is an approach to supervised learning that is used in statistics, data mining, and machine learning. In this form a classification or regression tree is used as a predictive model to draw conclusions about a set of observations. The goal of decision tree models is to create a model that can predict the value of a target variable based on several input variables. It's difficult to pinpoint the exact creator of decision trees, as not every algorithm is the same. Some of the most common decision tree algorithms are CART, ID3, C4.5, and CHAID.
    - In 1936 Ronald Fisher released his paper "Linear Discriminant Analysis".
    - 1980 saw Gordon V. Kass develop the CHAID (Chi-square automatic interaction detection) decision tree model.
    - The CART methodology was developed by Leo Brieman, Jerome Friedman, Richard Olshen, and Charles Stone in 1984.
    - In 1986, ID3 was developed by Ross J. Quinlan and published in his paper: "Induction of Decision Trees, Machine Learning". [26]
- The development of support vector machines (SVM) by Vladimir Vapnik and Alexey Chervonenkis in 1964, which offered a powerful technique for binary classification. [27] SVMs are a fast and dependable classification algorithm that performs very well with a limited amount of data to analyse. Compared to newer algorithms, such as neural networks, they have two advantages: higher speed and better performance with a limited number of samples.
- The invention of Bayesian networks by Judea Pearl in the 1980s, which provided a probabilistic framework for modelling complex relationships and reasoning under uncertainty. [28] Bayesian networks can define relationships between variables and therefore calculate probabilities. This makes them ideal for taking an event that occurred and predicting the likelihood that any one of several possible known causes was the contributing factor. Essentially, they model conditional dependence and therefore causation by representing conditional dependence.

Deep learning, a subset of machine learning, is focused on training multi-layer artificial neural networks. This method teaches computers to process data in a way that is inspired by the human brain. Much like the human brain contains millions of interconnected neurons that work together to learn and process information, deep learning neural networks are made of multiple layers of artificial neurons that work together inside the computer. Deep learning models can recognise complex patterns in pictures, text, sounds, and other data to produce specific insights and predictions and has been a driving force behind many of the most significant AI breakthroughs in recent years. Key milestones in deep learning include the following:

- The development of convolutional neural networks (CNNs) by Yann LeCun in the late 1980s, [29] which revolutionised computer vision tasks by efficiently learning hierarchical representations of images. CNNs use a mathematical operation called *convolution*, instead of general matrix multiplication, in one of their layers. They are specifically designed to process pixel data and, therefore, find their best use in image recognition and processing.
- The introduction of long short-term memory (LSTM) networks by Sepp Hochreiter and Jürgen Schmidhuber over the period of 1995 to '97, which enabled recurrent neural networks (RNNs) to learn long-range dependencies and improved their performance on sequence-to-sequence tasks. LSTM networks have been instrumental in the development of other platforms, with a notable one being Apple's Siri. [30]
- The invention of generative adversarial networks (GAN) by Ian Goodfellow in 2014, which provided a novel framework for generating realistic images, text, and other data by pitting two neural networks against each other. [31] It's a zero-sum game where one agent's gain is the other agent's loss. The two agents in a GAN are the generative network, which generates candidates, and the discriminative or discriminator network, which evaluates those candidates. The idea of a GAN is indirect training through the discriminator, which can tell how "realistic" the input seems.
- One of the most famous examples of GANs is the work of an artist called AI-Da, a robot artist who uses GANs to create unique drawings. The robot is programmed to understand and replicate different styles of art, from portraits to landscapes.

The advancements in AI techniques and algorithms have led to numerous breakthroughs and practical applications across various domains, including natural language processing, computer vision, and reinforcement learning. Some notable milestones include the following:

- IBM's Deep Blue defeating world chess champion Garry Kasparov in 1997. [32] At this point, chess-playing computers had existed since the 1950s. However, they had minimal success against skilled human players. Kasparov first played Deep Blue in 1996, and he was able to defeat the computer by switching his game strategy mid-way through the matchup. In 1997, his wait-and-see approach to his second match against Deep Blue is largely pointed to as the reason for his defeat match.
- Google's AlphaGo defeating world champion Go player Lee Sedol in 2016. [33] Go is an ancient Chinese board game where players take turns placing tiles on a board, trying to gain territory by arranging their tiles in strategic shapes. There are trillions of possible moves, making a strategy difficult to follow, and using intuition to react is the main way to master the game. The match was close, with AlphaGo and Sedol both making

mistakes. Ultimately Lee had to concede that AlphaGo had built an unattainable lead.

- OpenAI's GPT-3, a state-of-the-art language model capable of generating human-like text. [34] Generative Pretrained Transformer (GPT) -3 (third generation) is a neural network machine learning model trained using data from the internet to generate any type of text. It requires only a small amount of input text to generate large amounts of relevant machine-generated text. To put it into perspective GPT-3's deep learning neural network is a model with over 175 billion machine learning parameters. Prior to this, the Microsoft Turing Natural Language Generation (NLG) model was the largest neural network, with ten billion parameters. I always stress that GPT-3 and recently released GPT-4 are language prediction models. This means they can take text inputs and transform them into what they predict the most useful result will be. I find this to be a common misunderstanding amongst the wider public. GPT-3 and 4 don't know the answer; they simply predict the answer based on the input.

AI has had a transformative effect on the retail and e-commerce industries, enabling personalised shopping experiences, more efficient inventory management, and advanced customer service solutions. [35] By collecting large swathes of consumer data and feeding them into machine learning algorithms, retailers can develop detailed AI-powered personalisation, recommendation, and automation features, all of which are commonplace throughout the shopping experience. Key AI applications in retail and e-commerce include the following:

- The use of recommendation engines to provide personalised product suggestions based on customers' browsing history, preferences, and previous purchases. Amazon uses AI to help customers voice shop and get purchasing recommendations. Recommendation AI engines place greater emphasis on each individual customer rather than on an item. Therefore, they can piece together the history of a customer's shopping journey and serve them personalised product recommendations.
- The implementation of AI-driven chatbots and virtual assistants to provide instant customer support, answer questions, and handle complaints. *Chatbots* are automated programs used as a medium to interact with humans via textual or auditory means. They play a crucial role these days in customer service, where they acquire information from customers. A *virtual assistant*, on the other hand, is a digital personal software-based agent that can assist us in performing our daily activities, like setting a clock, scheduling an alarm, making calls, or typing messages, and so on.
- The application of machine learning algorithms for dynamic pricing, optimising prices in real time based on supply, demand, and market trends. Dynamic pricing is the practice of setting a price for a product or service based on current market conditions. Business reaps the benefits from a huge amount of data to understand and act upon any number of changing market conditions. Demand-based pricing sees prices grow

where there is an increase in consumer demand and limited supply or vice versa. AI is great at providing these processes, which require a large amount of market data to be captured and analysed. [36]

AI has also made its mark on the entertainment and media industries, enhancing content creation, discovery, and personalisation. Generative AI has democratised many aspects of content creation, opening up new ways to create written material, illustrations, sound effects, special effects, and more. Due to rapid maturation some have expressed concern this could be the end of creative professions. I believe the opposite is more likely: rather than making old models of creativity obsolete, AI is enabling new forms of expression, whether that is creating images or written content. Notable AI applications in entertainment and media include the following:

- The use of AI algorithms for automated content generation, such as creating news articles, video summaries, and even music compositions. Human guidance is still required here. Marketers must add descriptions, suggestions, and the tone of voice. AI content creation helps deliver enterprise data, customise descriptions, and adjust content on consumer behaviour according to their inputs.
- The application of AI-driven recommendation systems for content discovery and personalisation, enabling platforms like Netflix, Spotify, and YouTube to provide tailored suggestions to users. These AI systems use a machine learning algorithm that is trained to rank or rate content. It's designed to predict ratings a user might give to a specific item and then return those predictions to a user in the form of a ranked list.
- The integration of AI tools for enhancing video game experiences, with advanced Non Player Character (NPC) behaviour, procedural content generation, and adaptive difficulty levels. [37]

AI has significant potential in the fields of agriculture and environmental conservation, enabling more sustainable farming practices, improved crop management, and better monitoring of ecosystems, whether it's maximising yields from fruit, vegetables, or livestock or gathering data on the factors that influence these yields, including weather, temperature, or soil composition. Key AI applications in these domains include the following:

- The use of AI-powered drones and satellite imagery for precision agriculture, providing farmers with detailed information about crop health, soil conditions, and irrigation needs. It is possible to combine in-ground sensor data of moisture, fertiliser, and natural nutrient levels to analyse growth patterns as well as use visual data captured via drones.
- The application of machine learning algorithms for predicting crop yields and optimising resource allocation, leading to more efficient and sustainable farming practices. AI and machine learning are being used to reduce domestic and wild animals' potential to accidentally destroy crops or prevent break-ins on remote farms. Machine learning–based

surveillance systems are programmed or trained to identify employees who work on-site.

- The integration of AI tools for wildlife conservation, such as using computer vision algorithms to monitor animal populations and detect poaching activities. From camera traps and satellite imagery to audio recording, AI can learn how to identify which photo contains a rare species or pinpoint a specific animal call from hours of audio recording. AI is also used as a virtual fence, with thermal cameras tracking vehicle and human movement in an effort to reduce poaching of animals. [38]

AI is playing an increasingly important role in public safety and security, with applications ranging from crime prediction to disaster management. AI-enhanced technologies are also used for crowd estimation and weapon detection, identifying critical hardware failures and even reducing congestion to improve the flow of people and/or vehicles. Video analytics give machines the ability to label data quicker and more accurately, which in turn makes it easier to identify people, objects, or moments for use in the cases outlined above. In an emergency, time is of the essence, and these data insights have the potential to be lifesaving for first responders and civilians in and around the area of concern. Notable AI applications in public safety and security include the following:

- The use of AI algorithms for predictive policing, identifying crime hotspots and allocating resources more effectively to reduce criminal activity. Whilst this is a controversial point, it has important implications for cities and societies. The reason for AI and predictive policing being of concern is that it relies on AI and machine learning to record and map biometrics and facial recognition as well as smart cameras and community-wide public surveillance systems. People are increasingly aware that they are or may be tracked when out in public, and it is unnerving to some when it comes to how much privacy they are unknowingly giving up. We will explore privacy and ethics in AI later in the book. [39]
- The implementation of AI-driven facial recognition and object detection systems for improved surveillance and security in public spaces. Surveillance systems these days can detect and classify humans and objects, which can give insights into human actions relating to objects, i.e., the reason behind their actions and what has triggered a response. [40]
- The application of AI tools for disaster management, such as using machine learning algorithms to predict natural disasters, assess damages, and optimise emergency response efforts. [41] AI systems can be trained using seismic data on the magnitude and patterns of earthquakes to predict future locations of earthquakes and aftershocks. AI-based applications are being developed using rainfall records and flood simulations to predict and monitor flooding. AI can also utilise satellite data to predict and monitor the paths and intensity of hurricanes and tornadoes.

These breakthroughs and applications, ranging from healthcare diagnostics to autonomous driving and from language translation to content creation, cogently demonstrate the vast potential of AI to transform various aspects of our lives. The proliferation of AI is not just a testament to technological advancement, but an epoch where new possibilities are continually being unlocked and existing processes are undergoing rapid metamorphoses.

One of the intrinsic values of AI is its ability to analyse vast amounts of data at a scale impossible for humans, thereby creating opportunities for insights and efficiencies previously unattainable. This becomes particularly powerful in sectors like healthcare, where AI can help in early disease detection, or in agriculture, where it can predict yield and optimise resources.

As AI continues to evolve, we must recognise the multifaceted nature of this evolution. It is not just about algorithms becoming more advanced; it's also about AI becoming more accessible, adaptable, and capable of interweaving with various domains. This omnipresence of AI warrants a balanced approach to its development and application.

[17] https://bdtechtalks.com/2019/11/18/what-is-symbolic-artificial-intelligence/

[18] https://history-computer.com/logic-theorist/#:~:text=In%201955%2C%20Simon%20and%20Newell,and%20Bertrand%20Russell's%20Principia%20Mathematica.

[19] http://web.cse.ohio-state.edu/~stiff.4/cse3521/gps.html#:~:text=The%20General%20Problem%20Solver%20(GPS,written%20with%20very%20specific%20goals.

[20] https://www.cs.unm.edu/~williams/cs357/lecture2.pdf

[21] https://towardsdatascience.com/symbolic-vs-connectionist-a-i-8cf6b656927

[22] https://news.cornell.edu/stories/2019/09/professors-perceptron-paved-way-ai-60-years-too-soon

[23] https://www.linkedin.com/pulse/history-neural-networks-datta-dharanikota/

[24] http://www.scholarpedia.org/article/Hopfield_network#:~:text=Hopfield%20Networks%20%5BHopfield%201982%5D%20are,be%20either%20discrete%20or%20continuous.

[25] https://www.historyofdatascience.com/decision-tree-and-random-forest-algorithms-decision-drivers/

[26] https://holypython.com/dt/decision-tree-history/

[27] https://en.wikipedia.org/wiki/Support_vector_machine

[28] https://www.theatlantic.com/technology/archive/2018/05/machine-learning-is-stuck-on-asking-why/560675/

[29] https://www.historyofdatascience.com/yann-lecun/

[30] https://medium.com/mlearning-ai/building-a-neural-network-zoo-from-scratch-the-long-short-term-memory-network-1cec5cf31b7

[31] https://medium.com/syncedreview/father-of-gans-ian-goodfellow-splits-google-for-apple-279fcc54b328#:~:text=Goodfellow's%20most%20notable%20contribution%20is,the%20Generator%20from%20real%20data

[32] https://www.history.com/this-day-in-history/deep-blue-defeats-garry-kasparov-in-chess-match

[33] https://www.theguardian.com/technology/2016/mar/09/google-deepmind-alphago-ai-defeats-human-lee-sedol-first-game-go-contest

[34] https://openaimaster.com/capabilities-and-limitations-of-gpt-3-language-model/#:~:text=OpenAI's%20GPT%2D3%20(Generative%20Pre,lot%20of%20buzz%20since%20then

[35] https://www.vaimo.com/blog/ai-in-ecommerce/#:~:text=AI%20enables%20an%20ecommerce%20website,were%20interacting%20with%20a%20person.

[36] https://www.theaidream.com/post/price-optimisation-using-dynamic-pricing-and-machine-learning

[37] https://www.infosysbpm.com/blogs/media-entertainment/use-of-ai-in-media-entertainment-industry.html#:~:text=And%20when%20streaming%20in%20real,advertisements)%20and%20increase%20profit%20margins.

[38] https://encyclopedia.pub/entry/16111

[39] https://www.securityinfowatch.com/video-surveillance/article/53026728/how-ai-is-transforming-safety-and-security-in-public-places

[40] https://www.deloitte.com/an/en/Industries/government-public/perspectives/urban-future-with-a-purpose/surveillance-and-predictive-policing-through-ai.html

[41] https://glair.ai/post/how-ai-predictive-analysis-detect-natural-disaster#:~:text=And%20now%2C%20researchers%20have%20found,death%20for%20thousands%20of%20people.

AI's Impact on Society and the Economy

As we progress further into the digital era, the transformative effects of artificial intelligence on society and the economy are becoming increasingly pronounced. AI has revolutionised the very fabric of our daily lives, reshaping how we work, communicate, and engage with technology. In the previous chapter, we embarked on an exploration of AI's key breakthroughs and its potential in diverse industries. We will extend this exploration in the current chapter, scrutinising the multifaceted impacts of AI across various sectors, along with the opportunities and challenges that this ground-breaking technology presents.

One of the sectors in which AI has been a game-changer is healthcare. Artificial intelligence is making waves in the medical field, enabling improved diagnostics, paving the way for personalised medicine, and revolutionising drug discovery processes. The incorporation of AI into healthcare has the potential to dramatically enhance the delivery and effectiveness of medical services, ultimately leading to better patient outcomes.

Key advancements in AI-driven healthcare include the following:

- The use of deep learning algorithms for medical image analysis, which has significantly improved the accuracy and speed of disease detection in radiology, pathology, and other fields. [42] Applying AI to imaging data can also identify the thickening of certain muscle structures as well as monitor blood flow through the heart and associated arteries. AI has shown impressive accuracy and sensitivity in the identification of imaging abnormalities and promises to enhance tissue-based detection and characterisation.

- The application of AI in genomics and precision medicine, allowing for the development of tailored treatment plans based on individual patients' genetic profiles. [43] Precision medicine is about designing and optimising the pathway for diagnosis, therapeutic intervention, and prognosis by using large multidimensional biological datasets that capture individual variability in genes, function, and environment. This gives clinicians the ability to more carefully tailor early interventions, whether treatment or preventative measures, to each individual patient. AI algorithms can now achieve reasonable success in predicting risk in certain cancers and cardiovascular disease from available multidimensional clinical and biological data.

- The integration of AI-powered chatbots and virtual assistants in telemedicine, providing remote access to healthcare services and support. [44] There are several broad categories that incorporate AI. Remote patient monitoring, where AI and more specifically machine learning is being used in remote patient monitoring, receives and analyses patients' vital signs and alerts relevant parties to abnormal readings. AI is used to analyse data from blood pressure cuffs, heart monitors, and other medical devices to watch for anomalies. Using both individual patient data and larger sets of historical data, AI assists clinicians in reaching more accurate diagnoses and accurately interpreting the results of medical imaging and X-rays. AI-driven technologies such as chatbots streamline services such as providing information, scheduling appointments, and handling intake and reception prior to clinical visits. Chronic disease management is also reaping benefits from AI, like smart diabetes monitors, and providing feedback to patients and alerting them to early warning signs of disease progression.

In the financial sector, AI has facilitated more accurate risk assessment, streamlined customer service, and improved fraud detection. Notable AI applications in finance include the following:

- The implementation of machine learning algorithms for credit scoring, enabling lenders to make more informed decisions about loan approvals and interest rates. [45] AI and machine learning can analyse a wider range of data, including non-traditional data sources such as social media activity and utility bill payments, to develop a more accurate picture of a borrower's creditworthiness. Traditional credit scoring models can be limiting for individuals with thin credit files or non-traditional sources of income. AI and machine learning credit scoring models can also automate many parts of the lending process, reducing the need for manual underwriting and improving operational efficiency. This all contributes to more accurate credit scores, better loan decisions, and a better borrower experience.
- The use of AI-powered robo-advisors for personalised investment recommendations and portfolio management. [46] Algorithms are already doing a stellar job of dispensing basic investment advice, but the holy grail is to deliver holistic advice without human assistance. Financial adviser numbers have been falling, and the cost of advice is rising, making face-to-face advice unaffordable for many people. AI can plug this gap by providing "client-led" digital advice that is in the best interest of each user. Singular topics where AI is being utilised include salary sacrificing into superannuation funds, investment allocation, and saving and investment planning. Users can submit investment-related queries on listed companies' markets and stock insights and get information and answers within seconds.
- The deployment of AI systems to detect unusual patterns and prevent fraudulent transactions in real-time. [47] The statistics around online fraud are alarming. Studies show cybercrime costs the world economy $600 billion . . . annually. AI makes fraud detection faster, more reliable, and more efficient where traditional fraud detection models fail. AI-powered systems can process vast amounts of data faster and more accurately, which reduces the error margin in identifying normal and fraudulent customer behaviour, authenticates payments faster, and provides analysts with actionable insights. AI can detect and flag anomalies in real-time banking transactions, app usage, payment methods, and other

financial activities. Rule-based solutions, on the other hand, can only detect anomalies that they are programmed to identify. Machine learning algorithms self-learn by processing historical data and continuously identify evolving fraud patterns. Machine learning can also build predictive models to mitigate fraud risk with minimal human intervention.

AI has significantly optimized manufacturing processes and supply chain management, leading to increased efficiency, reduced costs, and enhanced product quality. Key AI contributions in this domain include the following:

- The integration of AI-driven robotics and automation systems in manufacturing facilities, allowing for greater precision and consistency in production. [48] Thorough quality control systems like machine vision manufacturing can benefit from an AI's precise evaluation of every product that goes through an assembly line—even before these goods and services find their way into the customer's hands. New product designs, for instance, can be developed through the combination of AI and engineering. Smart self-driving cars and smart homes are examples of innovative ventures that rely on artificial intelligence.
- The use of AI algorithms for demand forecasting and inventory optimization, enabling companies to reduce stockouts and overstocking. [49] Forecasting, making projections, and inventory planning are necessary steps for efficient manufacturing companies. Implementing AI platforms, such as machine learning, can help improve inventory management through efficiency, accuracy, and cost-effectiveness, especially when compared to traditional forecasting methods.
- The application of AI in predictive maintenance, allowing for the early detection of equipment failures and reducing downtime. [50] *Predictive maintenance* refers to the ability to use volumes of data to anticipate and address potential issues before they lead to breakdowns in operations, processes, services, or systems. Predictive maintenance can include benefits such as lowering costs by reducing unplanned downtime, fewer redundant inspections, and ineffective preventative maintenance measures; reduced equipment lifecycle costs through improved performance; and extended equipment life. Indirect benefits also include improved quality, reduced rework, reduced defects, improved safety, and increased energy efficiency.

In the realm of education, AI has the potential to revolutionize teaching and learning by providing personalised instruction, adaptive learning environments, and enhanced assessment tools. Noteworthy AI applications in education include the following:

- The development of AI-powered tutoring systems that provide personalised feedback and guidance to students based on their individual learning styles and progress. [51] Intelligent tutoring systems (ITSs) are computer systems that provide personalised instruction and feedback to students, often through the use of AI. They provide one-on-one curriculum, and by using deep learning algorithms, they can suggest certain study strategies for each individual student.

- The use of AI algorithms to create adaptive learning platforms that adjust content and pacing according to each student's needs and performance. [52] Adaptive learning has become more refined and effective due to advances in cloud-based computing power, scalability, and machine learning. It is characterised by intelligent adjustment of content, questions and answer choices based on performance, self-paced study, optimal individualised learning pathways, immediate feedback, and remediation. Adaptive learning using AI and machine learning can more accurately replicate the one-on-one instructor experience. It can leverage network knowledge maps to create knowledge and behavioural nodes, forming deeper relationships between content, learning objectives, and persona types. This powers a more efficient and effective learning experience, enabling complex real-time adaptations based on learner performance and behaviour, predictive insights into future knowledge application, and a reduction in learning times.

- The integration of AI tools for automated grading and assessment, reducing the workload for educators and allowing them to focus on more high-level tasks. [53] AI is playing a vital role in revolutionising exam evaluation through automated grading systems. Natural language processing (NLP) algorithms enable automated grading systems to analyse and evaluate written responses. AI can access the quality, coherence, and relevance of students answers. Pattern recognition is also used to recognise patterns in students' responses and identify common errors or misconceptions. This allows educators to pinpoint areas where students may be struggling and tailor their teaching strategies accordingly. AI can also generate detailed feedback for students and highlight their strengths and improvement areas. This feedback guides students but also saves educators time.

AI has played a significant role in transforming transportation and mobility, with advancements in autonomous vehicles, traffic management, and logistics. Key AI innovations in transportation include the following:

- The development of self-driving cars and trucks, which have the potential to improve road safety, reduce congestion, and revolutionize the logistics industry. [54] Self-driving vehicles use vast amounts of data, including image recognition systems, machine learning, and neural networks, to build systems that can drive autonomously. The neural networks identify patterns in the data which are then fed to the machine learning algorithms. That data includes images from cameras on self-driving cars from which the neural network learns to identify traffic lights, trees, curbs, pedestrians, street signs, and other parts of any given driving environment. Sensors, lidar, and cameras all feed the machine learning algorithm, which identifies everything around the vehicle and predicts what those objects might do next. The more the system drives, the more data it can feed into its deep learning algorithm to make more informed decisions in the future.

- The use of AI algorithms for real-time traffic prediction and management, leading to more efficient routing and reduced travel times. [55] For emergency vehicles, even lights and sirens can't help in peak-hour traffic. Route optimisation can allow quick passage for these vehicles. Real-time data from road surveillance cameras can be collected to detect disobedience of traffic rules. Dynamic traffic light sequencing using RFID allows real-time analysis and automation of traffic lights. This avoids traffic queues due to static sequencing when there may be no opposing traffic. Smart parking systems can help drivers find a parking spot quicker, and predictive analysis can notify drivers of occupancy levels in parking lots.
- The integration of AI-powered drones and autonomous delivery robots for last-mile logistics, providing faster and more cost-effective delivery services. [56] AI and machine learning are positively impacting last-mile logistics issues by optimising delivery routes, managing real-time tracking, and enabling efficient resource allocation. Autonomous vehicle delivery could transform the last mile delivery cost model. Urban warehouses are not common, but with micro fulfillment centres popping up everywhere, the distance between goods and customers is now closer than it has ever been, allowing for autonomous vehicles to assist in this process.

AI's impact on the job market and the future of work has been a topic of much debate and speculation. While AI has the potential to automate many routine tasks, it also creates opportunities for new jobs, industries, and skill sets. Some key considerations related to AI and the future of work include the following:

- The potential displacement of jobs due to automation, particularly in sectors with high levels of routine, manual, and repetitive tasks. [57] Through the recent pandemic we've seen an increase in AI-related displacement and redefinition of work. This will continue to rise moving forward. The World Economic Forum believes a quarter of all jobs will be affected over the next five years. The fast-growing trends of artificial intelligence, digitisation, renewable energy, and supply chain reshoring will bring about a critical shift in the global labour market. Many workers won't have the required skills to keep up with these changes.
- The emergence of new job opportunities in AI-related fields, such as data science, machine learning engineering, and AI ethics. [58] AI ethicists will see huge demand, as companies will want to ensure that their use of generative AI is responsible and ethical. *Prompt engineer* is a new and emerging job role and refers to a person who designs and creates prompts for large language models (LLMs). Prompts are instructions that tell LLMs what to do and can be used to generate text, translate languages, write creative content, and generate images and videos. AI auditors are already in demand as bias in AI platforms gains a lot of headlines. AI auditors will evaluate AI systems to ensure they work as

expected without bias or discrimination and are aligned with ethical and legal standards.

- The need for reskilling and upskilling programs to help workers adapt to the changing job landscape and acquire the necessary skills to thrive in an AI-driven economy. [59] Whilst AI can assist with certain tasks in the knowledge work fields (white collar roles) it's important to remember humans are still needed to operate and manage these systems. Areas that are relevant to upskill in include the following: data analysis and interpretation; understanding machine learning computer programming in such languages like Python and Java, as well as ethics; and understanding the impact of AI on society and how to use it responsibly can help people stay relevant in the job market.

- The importance of fostering human-AI collaboration, which can lead to improved productivity and better decision-making, as humans and machines leverage their complementary strengths. [60] Understanding these different weaknesses and strengths, AI and humans can work collaboratively and have been doing so for years with great results. Human-AI collaboration can lead to increased efficiency, and AI can automate repetitive tasks, provide data-driven insights, and lead to better decision-making. AI and humans can help businesses optimise costs and automate tasks. By working together, humans can provide context and decision-making abilities whilst AI provides data-driven information.

- The need for policymakers, educators, and industry leaders to work together to create a supportive ecosystem that prepares individuals for the future of work, including the development of robust educational programs, lifelong learning initiatives, and workforce transition support. [61] There are any number of stats out there on the internet about job losses, jobs being offset, or generally just how large the restructuring of knowledge work will be in the face of AI advances. Governments need to develop strategic frameworks, initiatives, and policies to help guide entire economies through an unprecedented period of technological change. Support will be needed for those who could experience job losses due to technology, and funds need to be kept aside for their support, retraining, and upskilling if we are to mitigate job losses over the next five to ten years. Universal basic income could be a topic we see reignite in the future to help ease the burden on societies if and when job losses start to ramp up due to AI.

- The ethical and social considerations related to AI and the future of work, such as addressing income inequality, ensuring fair access to opportunities, and promoting diversity and inclusion in AI-related fields. [62] AI may not reduce overall employment; however, it could reduce the relative amount of income going to low-skilled labour, which will increase inequality across society. Everyone will have a responsibility to ensure AI is responsible and trustworthy. Since communities are ultimately the producers of data and knowledge that allow AI systems to run, it makes sense to include their voices in the design phase of AI.

As we conclude this chapter, the expansive and complex impact of artificial intelligence on society and the economy becomes increasingly evident. AI's rapid advancement and penetration into various aspects of our lives present a panoply of both opportunities and challenges. From transforming industries and driving economic growth to reshaping job markets and introducing ethical dilemmas, AI is a potent force that is reshaping the contours of our society and economy.

The opportunities presented by AI are significant. AI-driven automation and data analysis can increase productivity, drive efficiency, and facilitate innovation across numerous sectors. From healthcare and education to finance and transportation, AI holds the promise of profoundly transforming our societal and economic structures, resulting in improved services, novel solutions, and even entirely new industries.

However, these opportunities are not without challenges. Job displacement due to AI-driven automation, data privacy concerns, the digital divide, and ethical questions surrounding AI decision-making are just a few of the complex issues that emerge as AI continues to advance. Addressing these challenges requires thoughtful, proactive, and concerted efforts from individuals, organisations, and governments.

As AI continues to evolve and become increasingly integrated into our lives, it is crucial for us, as a society, to harness the potential of this transformative technology to drive positive change. To do this, we must develop strategic frameworks and policies that promote the responsible and equitable use of AI. These might include investing in education and skills training to prepare for AI-driven job market changes, implementing robust data protection regulations, and promoting digital equity to ensure that the benefits of AI are accessible to all.

At the same time, in our pursuit of progress and innovation, we must remain mindful of the importance of preserving our humanity in an increasingly automated world. This involves promoting ethical AI development and use, ensuring that AI systems are transparent and accountable, and fostering a culture that values human uniqueness and prioritises human-centric design in AI technologies.

In the end, the journey of navigating the AI-driven society and economy is complex and multi-dimensional, requiring the balance of embracing the transformative potential of AI and preserving the essential qualities that make us human.

As we move into the next chapters, we will delve deeper into understanding the specific ways we can maintain our humanity in the age of AI. We will explore themes like emotional intelligence, the cultivation of creativity, and the importance of lifelong learning. Each of these elements will play a crucial role in ensuring that as we harness the benefits of AI, we continue to value and uphold our uniquely human traits and principles.

[42] https://link.springer.com/article/10.1007/s11042-021-10707-4

[43]https://www.ncbi.nlm.nih.gov/pmc/articles/PMC7877825/#:~:text=Precision%20 medicine%20methods%20identify%20phenotypes,decision%20making%20through %20augmented%20intelligence.

[44] https://telemedicine.arizona.edu/blog/how-ai-helps-physicians-improve-telehealth-patient-care-real-time

[45] https://www.datrics.ai/credit-scoring-using-machine-learning

[46] https://www.forbes.com/sites/garydrenik/2022/11/30/startup-uses-ai-to-deliver-custom-investment-portfolios-and-usher-in-wealth-30/?sh=cb35d8de6d51

[47] https://www.analyticssteps.com/blogs/how-ai-used-fraud-detection

[48] https://www.turing.com/resources/ai-in-automating-production-processes

[49] https://www.forbes.com/sites/forbestechcouncil/2023/02/06/5-ways-ai-can-benefit-demand-forecasting-and-inventory-planning/?sh=7e62ca38742a

[50] https://www.turing.com/resources/ai-in-automating-production-processes

[51] https://www.cmu.edu/news/stories/archives/2020/may/intelligent-tutors.html

[52] https://www.linkedin.com/pulse/revolutionising-education-ai-powered-adaptive-systems-mark/

[53] https://elearningindustry.com/artificial-intelligence-new-role-in-education-automated-paper-grading

[54] https://dataconomy.com/2022/12/28/artificial-intelligence-and-self-driving/

[55] https://www.clickworker.com/customer-blog/artificial-intelligence-road-traffic/

[56] https://futuramo.com/blog/from-drones-to-robots-the-latest-last-mile-delivery-innovations-you-cant-afford-to-ignore/

[57] https://www.axios.com/2023/03/29/robots-jobs-chatgpt-generative-ai

[58] https://www.forbes.com/sites/joemckendrick/2017/12/18/artificial-intelligence-is-creating-new-and-unconventional-career-paths/?sh=54914f2e578c

[59] https://www.linkedin.com/pulse/importance-upskilling-reskilling-age-automation-edustation-official/

[60] https://www.deloitte.com/an/en/our-thinking/insights/topics/talent/human-capital-trends/2020/human-ai-collaboration.html

[61] https://www.mckinsey.com/featured-insights/future-of-work/ai-automation-and-the-future-of-work-ten-things-to-solve-for

[62] https://www.mckinsey.com/featured-insights/future-of-work/ai-automation-and-the-future-of-work-ten-things-to-solve-for

CHAPTER 2: EMBRACING OUR UNIQUENESS

Human Traits that Differentiate Us from AI

As we continue our journey into an era where artificial intelligence becomes increasingly advanced and seamlessly integrated into our daily lives, we must pause and reflect on our place in this swiftly evolving landscape. At this juncture, it becomes crucial to identify, celebrate, and nurture the unique human traits that set us apart from AI. These traits not only constitute the essence of our humanity, but also serve as the beacon guiding us through the sweeping technological change.

In this chapter, we'll delve into an exploration of the distinct attributes that render us human, and which AI, no matter how advanced, cannot replicate. We'll explore the rich and multi-dimensional realms of creativity, empathy, intuition, and adaptability—traits that contribute to our unique human identity and experience.

Creativity, the ability to produce original thoughts and ideas, allows us to envision and innovate, paving the way for advancements in every field from arts and culture to science and technology. *Empathy*, our capacity to understand and share the feelings of others, enables deep connections and fosters cooperation, laying the foundations of our social structures. *Intuition*, our inherent ability to understand something instinctively, without the need for conscious reasoning, guides us in uncertain and complex situations. And adaptability, the ability to adjust to new conditions, equips us to navigate the ever-changing dynamics of our world.

In AI's ever-expanding presence, we might be tempted to measure human potential against AI's capabilities, but this comparison overlooks the inherent value of our uniquely human traits. These traits are not a mere list of attributes, but the vibrant threads that weave the tapestry of human existence. Therefore, nurturing these qualities is not a concession to our human limitations in the face of AI's advancements, but rather an affirmation of our irreplaceable worth and the resilience of the human spirit.

This chapter aims to illuminate the importance of these human characteristics in a world progressively captivated by AI. It also hopes to inspire a newfound appreciation for these traits and offer ways to nurture them in our lives. By doing so, we can ensure that our humanity remains the beating heart of our technological future, radiating its warmth and wisdom amidst the cool precision of our silicon counterparts.

While AI has made remarkable progress in generating content and even art, human creativity remains a unique and vital asset. Humans possess the innate ability to think outside the box, make connections between seemingly unrelated ideas, and generate original, innovative solutions. By fostering our creativity, we can continue to push the boundaries of what is possible and ensure that technology serves as a tool for human expression and ingenuity rather than a replacement for it. [63]

Empathy, or the ability to understand and share the feelings of others, is a fundamental human quality that sets us apart from AI. *Emotional intelligence*, which encompasses empathy and the ability to recognise and manage our own emotions, is another critical human trait. While AI systems can be programmed to recognise and respond to emotions, they cannot truly experience them. By nurturing our empathy and emotional intelligence, we can build more compassionate societies and ensure that technology is designed and used in a manner that supports human well-being. [64]

Intuition, or the ability to understand something instinctively without the need for conscious reasoning, is another uniquely human attribute. While AI can analyse vast amounts of data and identify patterns, human intuition allows us to make leaps of understanding and decision-making in complex, uncertain situations where data may be limited or contradictory. By valuing and honing our intuitive abilities, we can complement AI's data-driven insights and navigate the challenges of an increasingly complex world. [65]

Humans have a remarkable ability to adapt to new situations and learn from experience, often with limited information. While AI systems can be trained to perform specific tasks and adapt within predefined parameters, they typically struggle with novel situations that fall outside their training data. By cultivating our adaptability and ability to learn from experience, we can maintain our relevance in an ever-changing world and ensure that we can tackle unforeseen challenges.

Our social and cultural intelligence, or the ability to understand and navigate complex social situations and cultural contexts, is another human trait that distinguishes us from AI. While AI systems can be programmed to recognise social cues and mimic human behaviour, they lack a deep understanding and appreciation of the nuances of human interaction and cultural diversity. By fostering our social and cultural intelligence, we can create more inclusive societies and ensure that technology is developed and used in a manner that respects and celebrates human diversity.

In conclusion, as we continue to advance and integrate AI into our lives, it is crucial to embrace and nurture the unique human traits that differentiate us from AI. By doing so, we can ensure that our technology serves as a tool to enhance and support our humanity rather than diminish or replace it. In the following chapters, we will explore practical strategies for cultivating these human qualities and discuss the importance of education, ethics, and collaboration in shaping a future where humans and AI coexist harmoniously.

[63] https://www.forbes.com/sites/bernardmarr/2023/03/27/the-intersection-of-ai-and-human-creativity-can-machines-really-be-creative/?sh=7eaf6f273dbc

[64] https://hbr.org/2017/02/the-rise-of-ai-makes-emotional-intelligence-more-important

[65] https://uxdesign.cc/how-intuition-gives-humans-the-advantage-over-artificial-intelligence-3fd9c136b8f2

Creativity, Empathy, and Intuition

Undoubtedly, the essence of our humanity lies in our unique traits, such as creativity, empathy, and intuition. These qualities, while often overlooked in the face of technological progress, form the backbone of our identities and continue to differentiate us from AI. As we stand on the brink of an increasingly automated landscape, it becomes imperative to harness and nurture these inherent human traits, ultimately enabling us to thrive amidst the rapid advancements.

This chapter aims to delve deeper into the importance of these human attributes. We will unpack the nuances of creativity, empathy, and intuition, examining how these qualities contribute to our personal and professional lives. Moreover, we will provide practical strategies that can be implemented to cultivate these essential human traits.

Creativity, often seen as the cornerstone of human innovation and progress, plays a significant role in how we shape our world. It transcends traditional notions of artistic expression, seeping into our problem-solving abilities, our perspective on the world, and our approach to overcoming challenges. By embracing and nurturing our creative instincts, we can generate novel ideas, solve complex problems, and drive technological advancements in ways that AI's data-driven capabilities can't replicate.

Some practical strategies for fostering creativity include the following:

- Encouraging curiosity and open-mindedness: Nurture a mindset of exploration and inquisitiveness, allowing for the free flow of ideas and questioning of established norms. The power of being open-minded and curious is crucial to embrace new ideas and perspectives. Being open to new ideas and perspectives that differ from your own allows for a diverse range of influences and inspiration, leading to previously unthought-of and innovative solutions to problems. Curiosity also encourages exploration and experimentation—key components of creativity. [66]
- Providing opportunities for collaboration and diverse perspectives: Diverse teams can offer unique insights, challenge conventional thinking, and inspire creative solutions. [67] when it comes to unlocking innovation, workplace diversity and inclusion is the key. Regardless of industry, field, or domain, organisations that seek diverse viewpoints across ethnicity, gender, age, educational background, etc. experience higher rates of innovation. Diversity of thought broadens perspectives within an organisation and creates opportunities for a range of different mindsets, attitudes, and approaches. Diverse and inclusive teams create more unconventional ideas as inspiration is drawn from unrelated places based on the team members' differences in experience level, culture, age, educational background, etc. This expansive experience and resource base allows diverse teams to execute ideas more quickly, efficiently, and cost-effectively.

- Supporting risk-taking and experimentation: Emphasize the importance of learning from failure and iterating on ideas, allowing for creative growth and development. As the famous saying goes, "Everything you want is just outside your comfort zone". Put another way, everything you want requires some level of risk. Risk urges you to learn new skills and evolve already existing ones. Fear of failure is reduced once you embrace a risk-taking culture. Risk also encourages creative thinking, and in these fight-or-flight situations, you can really define your true objectives. [68]

Empathy, or the ability to understand and share the feelings of others, is a key component of our humanity. By cultivating empathy, we can forge meaningful connections, foster collaboration, and ensure that technology is designed and used in ways that prioritise human well-being. Some practical strategies for nurturing empathy include the following:

- Developing active listening skills: Practice truly hearing and understanding others' perspectives without judgement, fostering deeper connections and trust. [69] Active listening requires you to listen attentively to a speaker, understand what they are saying, and reflect on what's being said to then retain that information for later. This keeps both the listener and speaker actively engaged in the conversation. Too often people are listening whilst forming a rebuttal in their head. Active listening helps establish trust between parties. Being a thoughtful listener, asking questions, seeking clarification, and encouraging others to share their perspectives will help you build those connections with friends and colleagues as well as enhance the collaborative environment our societies are built upon. [69]
- Practicing perspective-taking: Put yourself in someone else's shoes to better understand their emotions, experiences, and motivations. A vast amount of scientific research suggests that perspective taking is crucial to human development and that it may lead to a variety of beneficial outcomes. Perspective-taking offers great opportunities to improve interpersonal relationships, workplace dynamics, and societies at large. At this point in time, I believe some social media algorithms give us personalised platforms that are merely echo chambers of our own perspective on life, so it can seem harder and harder to connect with people whose perspectives differ from our own. We need to learn how to understand the perspectives of others. Everyone views us differently from how we view ourselves. Differences in perspective are what cause some people to hold opposing views and can pit large groups of people against each other. If we learn to accept others' views by taking their perspectives, we can find common ground and build solutions that are mutually beneficial to all parties. [70]
- Engaging in empathy-building exercises: Participate in activities such as volunteering that encourage empathy and understanding of diverse experiences and backgrounds. Empathy is important, as it helps us understand how others are feeling so that we can respond appropriately to the situation. It helps us see past our differences and allows us to see

others who are of a different race, generation, or ideology than our own, without prejudice, stereotypes, or bias. Cultivating curiosity is a great way to develop your empathy. Spend time with people you don't know very well, ask them about themselves and what their life is like. Visit new places, travel, and immerse yourself in different cultures. Have difficult but respectful conversations. Don't shy away from hard topics, and be open to ideas that are new and different from your own. [71]

Intuition, or the ability to understand something instinctively without conscious reasoning, is another uniquely human trait that can complement AI's data-driven insights. By honing our intuition, we can make better decisions and navigate complex situations with limited or ambiguous information. Some practical strategies for cultivating intuition include the following:

- Embracing introspection and self-awareness: Regularly reflect on your thoughts, feelings, and experiences to develop a better understanding of your intuitive instincts. When we see ourselves clearly, we are more confident and more creative. Self-awareness means understanding your personality as well as your values, relationships, and beliefs. Do you like to reflect on what happens each day, or do you avoid thinking about your feelings? Self-awareness increases your ability to exercise control over your emotions by reducing stress and anxiety. [72]
- Practicing mindfulness and meditation: Engage in activities that promote mental clarity and focus, enabling you to better recognise and trust your intuitive insights. Mindfulness is the basic human ability to be present in the moment. In our increasingly tech-dominated society, this is becoming harder to achieve, as its quite easy in the "always on" mentality of today's society to become overwhelmed and overstimulated. Meditation, on the other hand, is a type of mind-body therapy. During meditation, you focus your mind on one particular thing, such as your breathing, body movements, and feelings. [73]
- Balancing analysis and intuition: Learn to integrate data-driven insights with your intuitive understanding, leveraging the strengths of both approaches to make well-informed decisions. Analysis is the process or act of studying and examining something in detail, breaking it down into smaller parts in order to discover or understand more about it. [74] Intuition is that feeling in your gut when you just know that something is right or wrong. It can be thought of as an insight that arises spontaneously without conscious reasoning. People rarely make decisions of intuition alone. When paired with analysis on a certain subject, a decision made with a mix of intuition and analysis of the subject could lead to more successful outcomes. [75]

The profound surge in artificial intelligence and automation underscores the imperative need to nurture and bolster the unique human traits that distinguish us, such as creativity, empathy, and intuition. These qualities, intrinsically tied to our humanity, serve as the bedrock of our resilience and adaptability in a fast-paced,

AI-driven world. By fostering these traits, we can ensure that our distinctive human essence continues to thrive amidst the rapidly evolving technological landscape.

In the forthcoming chapters, we will delve into the pivotal roles of education, ethics, and collaboration in cultivating and enhancing these unique human traits. We will navigate through an array of practical strategies and tangible approaches designed to develop and reinforce creativity, empathy, and intuition at all stages of our lives.

[66] https://www.verywellmind.com/be-more-open-minded-4690673

[67] https://www.fdmgroup.com/blog/how-diversity-of-thought-solves-business-challenges/

[68] https://www.elorus.com/blog/how-to-cultivate-a-risk-taking-culture-inside-your-company/

[69] https://www.mindtools.com/az4wxv7/active-listening

[70] https://ampcreative.com/what-is-perspective-taking/

[71] https://positivepsychology.com/empathy-worksheets/

[72] https://www.nirandfar.com/introspection/

[73] https://www.mindful.org/meditation/mindfulness-getting-started/

[74] https://en.wikipedia.org/wiki/Analysis

[75] https://positivepsychology.com/intuition/

The Role of Emotions in Decision-Making

Emotions play a significant role in human decision-making, providing valuable information and influencing our choices in complex and subtle ways. As artificial intelligence becomes more advanced and integrated into various aspects of our lives, it is essential to understand the importance of emotions in decision-making and cultivate the ability to balance rationality and emotion. In this chapter, we will explore the role of emotions in decision-making, the benefits and challenges associated with emotional decision-making, and practical strategies for achieving a balance between rationality and emotion.

Contrary to popular belief, emotions are not necessarily at odds with rational decision-making. In fact, emotions can provide crucial information about our preferences, values, and past experiences, helping us make choices that align with our goals and needs. Studies have shown that people with damage to the emotional processing regions of the brain struggle to make even simple decisions, highlighting the importance of emotions in decision-making processes. [76]

Emotional decision-making offers several benefits, such as the following:

- Enhanced intuition: Emotions can provide valuable insights into our subconscious understanding of situations, helping us make decisions based on gut feelings or instincts. An advantage of instinctive emotional decision-making is that it is quick. If you are in a time-sensitive situation, you don't want to waste time working through pros and cons. On the other hand, when faced with a choice about something completely insignificant, it's not the best use of time to spend hours deliberating over the seemingly insignificant everyday decisions. Decisions led by emotions can also be more compassionate, particularly when they affect other people. [77]
- Improved motivation and commitment: Emotional connections to decisions can lead to increased motivation and commitment to act on those choices. [78] Motivation is closely linked to emotions. A motivation is a driving force that initiates and directs behaviour. An emotion is a mental and physiological feeling that directs our attention and guides our behaviour. It's the emotions that you evoke within others or even yourself that enable you to bring out the best in them or direct your own behaviour.
- Strengthened relationships: Decisions made with empathy and emotional understanding can foster stronger connections with others and promote collaboration. [79] The power of emotion is often overlooked in corporate culture, but it is vital to an individual's motivation as well as building human connections with colleagues and employees to create a safe and innovative workplace. There are numerous studies and articles that detail the fact that employees who are motivated perform well, have greater job satisfaction, and can communicate effectively and influence others to establish an emotional climate around themselves of general well-being.

However, emotional decision-making also presents challenges, including the following:

- Biased judgements: Emotions can sometimes cloud our judgement, leading to decisions based on irrational fears, personal biases, or wishful thinking. [80] Emotional bias is a distortion in cognition and decision-making due to emotional factors. Emotions can also affect different types of decisions. Emotional biases typically occur spontaneously based on the personal feelings of an individual at the time a decision is made. They can also be deeply rooted in personal experiences that also affect decision-making.
- Short-term focus: Emotion-driven decisions may prioritise immediate emotional satisfaction at the expense of long-term goals or consequences. [81] The heat of the moment is a powerful yet sometimes dangerous thing. Much of the value of short-term goals is the emotional reward of moving forward quickly and feeling a sense of progress. When we make decisions with a short-term focus on getting things done, it can sometimes come at the expense of our long-term goals. The regret and consequences can last anywhere from days to weeks to years even.

To achieve a balance between rationality and emotion in decision-making, consider the following strategies:

- Cultivate self-awareness: Develop an understanding of your emotional triggers and tendencies, recognising how they may influence your decisions. [82] *Self-awareness* is the recognition of one's own emotional state at any given point in time. A lot of the time we can be totally oblivious to the emotional state we are in and the degree to which that state influences our behaviour and thought process. To cultivate and develop your self-awareness, you could try several things, including being curious about who you are and letting your walls down. When we see something we don't immediately like about ourselves, our first reaction is to defend ourselves from it. This is why becoming self-aware is so challenging. Try keeping a journal and note down what triggers positive feelings. Substitute screen time with people time. A big focus of mine is thinking about the amount of time we spend alone gazing at our screens. It wouldn't surprise me if it surpasses the time we spend in face-to-face interactions. We need time with people and friends to develop our sense of self. The biggest tip I've received on self-awareness is to just check in with yourself: "How am I feeling? What do I think is driving that feeling?"
- Practice mindfulness: Engage in mindfulness exercises to increase your ability to observe and manage your emotions, promoting clarity and focus in decision-making. [83] Mindfulness Is the quality of being present and fully engaged with whatever we're doing at that moment, free from distraction or judgement and aware of our thoughts and feeling without getting caught up in them. Mindfulness doesn't eliminate stress or other difficulties. Instead, by becoming aware of unpleasant thoughts and

emotions that arise because of challenging situations, we have more choice in how we handle them in the moment and a better chance of reacting calmly and empathetically.

- Encourage reflection and analysis: Take time to evaluate the pros and cons of different options and consider the potential consequences of your decisions. [84] Too often we succumb to the reward of the outcome, and in doing so we ignore the important parts of a decision. For example, have we considered the facts, the situation? Is any information incomplete as we make our decision? What about our biases and how the outcome could affect us or those around us? Reflection is the process of structured thinking to help you analyse your decision. It requires being open-minded and honest and using self-awareness to reflect on the decision-making process, not on the decision itself.

- Validate and acknowledge emotions: Recognise the emotions involved in a decision, validating their importance without allowing them to overshadow rational considerations. [85] Emotions shape decisions via depth of thought. In addition to influencing the content of thought, emotions also influence the depth of information processing related to the decisions we make. When we are faced with difficult decisions, we tend to experience a number of complex emotions. This can be uncomfortable, and we tend to get the decision-making over and done with as quickly as possible. Unfortunately, this often leads to poor decisions. To make better decisions, we need to identify the emotions we feel as we make the decision and the emotions we want to feel after we have made the decision.

- Seek diverse perspectives: Consult with others to gain additional insights and consider the emotional impact of decisions on all stakeholders involved. [86] Without thought, diversity innovation can be difficult and initiatives and pilot projects can stall, and overall, it can be difficult to sell ideas and plans without the inclusion of others. Seeking input is crucial to decision-making. Everyone wants to feel like they have been included or at least consulted in decisions that affect them. It's also worth remembering that whilst our egos would have us believe we have all the answers or our way is indeed the best way, our own perspectives, whilst valid and important, are limited by our own experiences.

The profound significance of understanding the role of emotions in our decision-making processes comes into sharp focus. In an era marked by the increasing integration of artificial intelligence into our daily lives, the ability to balance rationality and emotion is of paramount importance. By cultivating this balance, we are harnessing a unique human capacity—that of nuanced, empathetic, and effective decision-making—even as we navigate an increasingly AI-driven world.

Emotions, contrary to some views, are not antithetical to rationality. Rather, they provide a depth of understanding and a contextual lens that pure rationality may miss. They add nuance to our decisions, allow us to empathize with others, and ultimately make us effective decision-makers in complex, real-world situations. At the same time, rationality provides a critical counterbalance, ensuring that our decisions are not solely driven by transient emotions but are grounded in logical analysis and reasoning. Achieving a balance between these two facets of decision-making is a testament to the richness and complexity of human cognition.

Moreover, this balance is even more critical as we interact with and leverage artificial intelligence in our decision-making. AI, with its ability to analyse vast amounts of data and recognise patterns with superhuman speed and accuracy, brings a new dimension to rational decision-making. However, it lacks the capacity for emotional understanding and empathy, the uniquely human qualities that add depth and context to our decisions. Recognising this limitation of AI underscores the importance of human input and our emotional capabilities in the decision-making process.

However, understanding and balancing emotion and rationality in our decision-making is just one aspect of maintaining our humanity in the midst of AI's rise.

The chapters to follow will delve into additional strategies that collectively contribute to this overarching goal. We will explore the crucial role of education in shaping a future that both leverages AI's strengths and respects our human values. We will examine the ethical dimensions of AI and how we can ensure that AI technology is designed and used in a manner consistent with our collective moral principles. Furthermore, we will underscore the importance of collaboration—not just among humans, but also between humans and AI—as a way to ensure that the benefits of AI are maximized, its potential pitfalls mitigated, and its development and deployment guided by a human-centric perspective.

In conclusion, understanding the role of emotions and cultivating the ability to balance emotion with rationality, particularly in an AI-driven context, are crucial components of effective decision-making. Combined with education, ethical considerations, and collaboration, these elements will help us to maintain and cultivate our humanity in the rapidly advancing age of artificial intelligence. As we proceed on this journey, it becomes increasingly clear that these strategies are not just desirable, but essential for a future that respects and preserves our shared human experience.

[76] https://psychology.org.au/for-members/publications/inpsych/2020/aug-sept-issue-4/decisions,-decisions

[77] https://psychology.org.au/for-members/publications/inpsych/2020/aug-sept-issue-4/decisions,-decisions

[78] https://opentextbc.ca/introductiontopsychology/chapter/chapter-10-emotions-and-motivations/

[79] https://hbr.org/2022/07/motivating-people-starts-with-building-emotional-connections

[80] https://en.wikipedia.org/wiki/Emotional_bias#Decision_making

[81] https://hbr.org/2010/01/column-the-long-term-effects-of-short-term-emotions

[82] https://declutterthemind.com/blog/self-awareness/#:~:text=Ask%20yourself%20what%20made%20you,a%20closer%20look%20at%20them.

[83] https://en.wikipedia.org/wiki/Mindfulness

[84] https://medium.com/the-resolve-blog/reflection-helping-you-make-better-decisions-a3371b4f2791

[85] https://hbr.org/2022/09/emotions-arent-the-enemy-of-good-decision-making

[86] https://www.fierceinc.com/different-perspectives-lead-to-the-best-ideas-here-s-why/

CHAPTER 3: NURTURING EMOTIONAL INTELLIGENCE

The Importance of Emotional Intelligence

In our rapidly evolving technological landscape, where artificial intelligence (AI) plays an increasingly pervasive role, there remains a key human capability that shines through as distinctly irreplaceable: emotional intelligence (EI). This human faculty plays a pivotal role in both our personal and professional lives, acting as our compass in navigating complex social landscapes, forging resilient relationships, and making well-rounded, empathetic decisions.

Emotional intelligence, the ability to identify, use, understand, and manage emotions, is a quintessential aspect of our human nature. It brings depth to our interactions and allows us to connect with others on a deeply empathetic level, something that, despite its vast analytical capabilities, AI has yet to replicate. As we progress further into the AI era, recognising and nurturing our emotional intelligence becomes not only desirable but indispensable. It is a potent way to maintain our unique human edge in a world of growing automation.

In this chapter, we delve into the essentiality of emotional intelligence in the age of AI. We aim to underscore its value in enriching our personal lives, enhancing our professional endeavours, and even shaping our interactions with AI itself. We'll be exploring emotional intelligence from the perspective of its four core components: self-awareness, self-management, social awareness, and relationship management. Each of these components contributes to our overall emotional intelligence and informs how we relate to ourselves, others, and the world around us.

Moreover, we'll be sharing practical strategies for cultivating these aspects of emotional intelligence in our day-to-day lives. By providing you with these tools, we hope to enable you to further develop your EI, thereby reinforcing your human edge as we journey through the AI-dominated era.

As we step into the world of emotional intelligence, it's important to remember that it is not a skill to be attained but a continual process of understanding and growth. As such, it is perfectly suited to our human nature, adaptable and ever-evolving, capable of learning and development, much like our journey in this AI-integrated world.

Emotional intelligence consists of four main components: [87]

1. Self-awareness: The ability to recognise and understand our emotions and their impact on our thoughts and actions. [87] This is considered the foundation for all the other parts of emotional intelligence. Those with high levels of self-awareness learn to trust their "gut feelings" and realise these feelings can provide useful information about difficult decisions.

Understanding your own strengths and weakness and self-confidence are other markers of self-awareness.

2. Self-management: The ability to regulate and control our emotions, adapting to changing circumstances and coping with stress. [87] Those who can manage their emotions perform better because they are able to think clearly. Managing emotions does not mean suppressing or denying them but understanding them and using that understanding to deal with situations productively.

3. Social awareness: The ability to empathise with others and understand their emotions, needs, and perspectives. [87] Social awareness also includes understanding how to react to different social situations and effectively modify your interactions with other people so you can achieve the best results. It means being aware of the world around you and how different environments influence people. Increasing social awareness means improving your skills to connect with others verbally, nonverbally, and in the community.

4. Relationship management: The ability to build and maintain healthy relationships, effectively communicate, and resolve conflicts. [87] Relationship management includes the identification, analysis, and management of relationships with people inside and outside of your team, as well as their development. It is also vital in negotiating successfully, resolving conflicts, and working with others toward a shared goal.

Emotional intelligence is crucial for various aspects of our lives, including the following:

- Personal well-being: Developing EI can lead to improved mental and emotional well-being, better stress management, and increased resilience. Research suggests there is a strong connection between emotional intelligence and positive well-being. People under stress demonstrate lower EI and are unable to adopt positive methods and techniques required to minimise the negative effects of stress on physical and mental health. Emotional intelligence has been shown to impact positively on self-esteem, life satisfaction, and self-acceptance. [88]

- Effective decision-making: EI enables us to balance emotions and rational thinking, leading to more informed and effective decisions. Using your emotional intelligence to inform your decisions means being aware of what you are feeling when weighing up your choices. It also means being aware of how others around you will feel based on the decisions you make. [89]

- Enhanced communication: Emotional intelligence allows us to communicate more effectively, express our emotions clearly, and understand the emotions of others. Our emotions are directly connected to how we communicate. Managing your emotions better will help you communicate more effectively. With emotional intelligence, you can better understand the feelings and needs of others and respond in a way that meets their needs. Using your emotional intelligence, you can build stronger relationships, resolve conflicts, and influence others, all of which are elements of effective communication. [90]

- Stronger relationships: High EI helps us build and maintain healthy relationships by fostering empathy, understanding, and conflict resolution. By improving your self-awareness and social awareness, you make people around you feel welcome to speak about their feelings and thoughts by creating a safe atmosphere for your interactions. By clueing into the subtle and sometimes nonverbal language and cues, you can help people open up more in conversation. [91]
- Professional success: Emotional intelligence is linked to increased job satisfaction, improved leadership skills, and better team performance. Individuals with high EI tend to be self-motivated. Money or title does not drive them—a sense of ambition to self-drive and achieve and improve does: readiness to act on opportunities, a commitment to personal or company goals, and the ability to stay positive in the face of setbacks. They realise how their actions can affect other colleagues. They take feedback and criticism positively and are typically ready to learn from their mistakes. High EI also empowers positivity. People with a positive attitude don't hide from tough work, and they consider failure a chance to learn. Highly emotionally intelligent people don't run away in the face of change; they generally embrace it. They understand that change truly is the only constant in life. Success takes many forms and means many things to many people, but your emotional intelligence can help get you there a lot quicker. [92]

To develop emotional intelligence, consider implementing the following strategies:

- Practice self-reflection: Regularly reflect on your emotions, thoughts, and actions, developing a deeper understanding of your emotional landscape. Self-reflection is part of self-awareness. It's the practice of looking back on the day without bias or regret to contemplate your behaviour and consequences. It is taking an honest moment to think about what transpired, what worked, what didn't, what can be done, and what cannot. It is thoughtful and deliberate. Self-reflection takes courage; you may not always be happy with how you performed in that moment or in a certain situation, but it's how you grow and learn. Soft skills are what makes us human and the key theme of this book because, after all, technology such as artificial intelligence can't perform in the realm of soft skills. [93]
- Develop active listening skills: Improve your ability to listen and understand others' emotions and perspectives by practicing active listening and maintaining an open, non-judgemental mindset. Active listening involves five key elements: paying attention, showing that you are listening, providing feedback, summarising what was said, deferring judgement, and responding appropriately. [94]

- Engage in mindfulness exercises: Participate in mindfulness practices, such as meditation or deep breathing, to enhance emotional self-awareness and self-regulation. Some examples of exercises that can help with mindfulness include paying attention—slowing down and noticing things around you, living in the moment, and accepting yourself. Focusing on your breathing and various types of meditation can all be practiced anywhere, at any time. [95]
- Seek feedback from others: Ask for feedback from friends, family, and colleagues to gain insight into your emotional strengths and areas for improvement. When asking for feedback, make it clear that you want honest feedback so you can genuinely learn and grow. Focus on what you can do better in the future instead of what went wrong in the past. Ask questions and be specific about times or areas you feel you are. Ensure you listen and withhold judgment. Becoming defensive will make it less likely that the other person will be honest with you. [91]
- Strengthen empathy: Engage in empathy-building exercises, such as volunteering or community meetups, to develop your ability to understand and share the emotions of others. Acknowledge your own biases and move beyond your own worldviews to try to understand those held by other people. Start conversations with strangers or colleagues you don't normally work with. Conferences and networking events are great for this, where you have to engage in small talk and inadvertently learn about other people and their opinions. Stand up for others, and speak up when someone interrupts; this is important when you are not part of the community being undermined. These are just a few examples of exercises that could help you build your empathy in order to connect with people and situations that aren't part of your normal day-to-day life. [92]

As we bring this chapter to a close, it's important to emphasize the critical role that emotional intelligence plays in preserving our humanity amidst the rising tide of artificial intelligence. By developing and enhancing our emotional intelligence, we not only equip ourselves to navigate the complexities of our personal and professional lives more effectively, but we also pave the way for richer, more meaningful relationships, lending an added depth to our interactions.

Emotional intelligence—consisting of self-awareness, self-regulation, motivation, empathy, and social skills—provides the cornerstone of effective and empathetic communication, problem-solving, and decision-making. In the era of AI, these are the very skills that underscore our uniquely human edge, allowing us to complement and synergize with the strengths of artificial intelligence.

In the chapters that follow, we will delve deeper into additional strategies and methodologies to safeguard our human essence in an increasingly AI-centric world.

[87] https://p4s.pt/en/the-4-pillars-of-emotional-intelligence-and-why-they-matter/

[88] https://www.forbes.com/sites/colleenreilly/2023/06/20/is-your-emotional-intelligence-affecting-your-wellbeing/?sh=773f75e39658

[89] https://www.talentsmarteq.com/blog/decision-making-powered-by-emotional-intelligence/

[90] https://trainingindustry.com/articles/professional-development/effective-communication-skills-start-with-emotional-intelligence/

[91] https://www.intelligentchange.com/blogs/read/emotional-intelligence-and-its-role-in-relationships

[92] https://www.business.com/articles/5-ways-emotional-intelligence-predicts-your-success/

[93] https://toggl.com/track/self-reflection/#:~:text=Self%20reflection%20can%20help%20you,develop%20your%20sense%20of%20identity.

[94] https://www.acn.edu.au/thought-leadership/active-listening#active-listening-involves-five-elements

[95] https://www.mayoclinic.org/healthy-lifestyle/consumer-health/in-depth/mindfulness-exercises/art-20046356

[91] https://hbr.org/2015/05/how-to-get-the-feedback-you-need

[92] https://www.nytimes.com/guides/year-of-living-better/how-to-be-more-empathetic

Balancing Emotions and Artificial Intelligence in Decision-Making

Navigating the intricate dynamics of an AI-dominated landscape requires a deft interplay between artificial intelligence and our innate emotional intelligence. To ensure that we retain our human essence while leveraging the bounties of AI, we must actively cultivate our emotional intelligence, with its rich insights into understanding and managing emotions, while simultaneously harnessing AI's formidable prowess in generating data-driven insights for informed decision-making. In this chapter, we delve deeper into the critical importance of balancing emotional and artificial intelligence in decision-making, and we outline practical, actionable strategies to foster this balance.

Emotional intelligence (EI) and artificial intelligence (AI) bring to the table complementary strengths that, when effectively utilised, can significantly enrich the decision-making process. EI, with its focus on self-awareness, self-regulation, empathy, and social skills, facilitates a nuanced understanding of our emotional landscape and empowers us to make decisions anchored in our values and personal experiences and the human context.

Conversely, AI shines in its capacity to analyse vast volumes of data rapidly and accurately, drawing predictive insights and pinpointing patterns beyond human cognitive reach. It offers a robust, data-driven foundation for decision-making, and if set up, trained, and monitored properly can be free from the biases and errors that can creep into human judgement.

By marrying these two forms of intelligence, we can arrive at well-rounded decisions that effectively straddle the human and technological domains. This harmonious balance enables us to capture the essence of our humanity while also taking advantage of the precision and efficiency that AI offers. We can foster empathetic and ethical decisions that also stand up to the rigor of data-driven logic.

Weaving a robust tapestry of AI and EI requires strategic cultivation and active nurturing. This chapter outlines the various ways we can do this, including developing self-awareness, practicing emotional regulation, cultivating empathy, improving social skills, and learning how to leverage AI's capabilities effectively. By integrating these strategies into our lives, we can navigate the intricate dance between AI and EI, crafting a future where we harness the strengths of AI without compromising our unique human qualities.

Striking a balance between emotional and artificial intelligence in decision-making offers several benefits, including the following:

- Enhanced decision-making: Combining the strengths of EI and AI allows for more comprehensive, informed, and nuanced decision-making that accounts for both emotional and data-driven factors. [93]

- Improved adaptability: Leveraging the insights offered by both EI and AI can help us better navigate complex, rapidly changing environments and adapt to new challenges.
- Stronger relationships: Integrating emotional intelligence with AI-driven insights can foster empathy, understanding, and trust in interpersonal and professional relationships. [94]
- Ethical considerations: Balancing EI and AI can help ensure that technology is used responsibly and ethically, prioritising human well-being and considering the emotional impact of decisions. [95]

To achieve a balance between emotional and artificial intelligence in decision-making, consider the following strategies:

- Cultivate self-awareness: Develop a deeper understanding of your emotional landscape, recognising how emotions may influence your decisions and interactions with AI. [96]
- Validate and acknowledge emotions: Recognise the emotions involved in a decision, validating their importance without allowing them to overshadow data-driven insights provided by AI. [97] In an earlier chapter, we outlined how emotions can affect decision-making: emotion-driven decisions may prioritise immediate emotional satisfaction at the expense of long-term goals.
- Integrate data-driven insights with emotional understanding: Learn to combine the insights offered by AI with your intuitive understanding of emotions, values, and experiences. [98] Emotional intelligence and mastering our emotions has the potential to revolutionize the way we interact with technology. Whilst AI will uncover patterns in data that humans may not see straight away, our emotional nature helps us make meaningful and rational decisions with that data.
- Seek diverse perspectives: Consult with others to gain additional emotional insights, and consider the emotional impact of decisions on all stakeholders involved. All the data in the world means nothing if you don't have diversity of thought and perspective. As we all look at situations and data differently, we all have different perspectives that together can assist in understanding the full consequences of decisions through a much wider lens before any action is taken. [99]
- Continuously learn and adapt: Stay informed about advancements in AI and develop your emotional intelligence skills to better navigate the evolving relationship between humans and technology.

As we draw this chapter to a close, we underline the vital role of nurturing emotional intelligence and the importance of striking a harmonious balance between EI and AI in our decision-making processes. With the increasing integration of artificial intelligence in our daily lives, thriving in the AI era calls for leveraging the unique strengths of both human and technological intelligence. The amalgamation of empathy, self-awareness, and complex emotional understanding, inherent in humans, combined with the analytical and data-driven capabilities of AI, can lead to more informed, empathetic, and effective decisions that promote individual and societal well-being.

The distinct strengths of EI and AI can act in concert, complementing each other to foster a decision-making framework that is both powerful and humane. Emotional intelligence helps us navigate the human dimensions of our lives, understanding and managing our emotions, empathizing with others, and making morally informed decisions. On the other hand, AI can manage large volumes of data, recognise patterns, and make predictions, thereby aiding us in making more informed decisions.

However, fostering emotional intelligence and finding an equilibrium between EI and AI is just one aspect of preserving our humanity in the midst of the digital age. The upcoming chapters will delve deeper into other strategies that collectively help to achieve this goal.

We will also explore the importance of education in preparing us for an AI-driven future, enhancing our understanding of these technologies and their ethical implications, and nurturing a digitally literate society. We will delve into the ethical considerations surrounding AI, emphasizing the need to develop and adhere to ethical guidelines that ensure AI technology aligns with our shared human values and principles.

We will also discuss the role of collaboration. Collaboration between humans, and between humans and AI, can help ensure that technology serves us and enhances our lives. With such an approach, we can avoid the potential pitfalls of AI and maximize its benefits, creating a future where technology is our ally, not our adversary.

In summary, the balance between emotional intelligence and artificial intelligence is key to making effective decisions and maintaining our humanity in an AI-driven world. Along with emotional intelligence, education, ethics, and collaboration are critical elements in ensuring we thrive in the age of AI, while preserving the essence of what makes us truly human. As we continue our journey into the age of AI, it becomes ever more critical to understand, nurture, and leverage these elements for the benefit of our personal lives, our societies, and our shared human experience.

[93] https://www.linkedin.com/pulse/ai-meets-ei-vice-versa-piyali-shanker/

[94] https://www.linkedin.com/pulse/ai-meets-ei-vice-versa-piyali-shanker/

[95] https://www.linkedin.com/pulse/ai-meets-ei-vice-versa-piyali-shanker/

[96] https://www.nbcnews.com/better/lifestyle/what-self-awareness-how-can-you-cultivate-it-ncna1067721

[97] https://hbr.org/2022/09/emotions-arent-the-enemy-of-good-decision-making

[98] https://guptadeepak.com/ai-and-emotional-intelligence-a-look-into-the-future/#:~:text=Implications%20of%20AI%20and%20Emotional%20Intelligence&text=AI%20can%20also%20improve%20decision,way%20we%20interact%20with%20technology.

[99] https://www.fierceinc.com/different-perspectives-lead-to-the-best-ideas-here-s-why/

CHAPTER 4: CULTIVATING HUMAN CONNECTIONS

The Role of Human Interaction in a Digital World

As we traverse the landscape of a technology-dominated era, the essence of meaningful human connections becomes not only relevant but indispensable. The rapid advancements in technology, including AI and digital tools, offer remarkable conveniences and efficiencies, yet they fall short of replicating the unique depth and essence that characterizes human interactions. This realization underscores the fundamental truth that, no matter how far technology progresses, it cannot replace the value of genuine human connection. In this chapter, we will delve into the importance of human relationships in our increasingly digital society and explore strategies to foster and sustain them in the face of mounting technological immersion.

Human connections serve as the bedrock of our personal and social well-being, enriching our lives with shared experiences, mutual understanding, and a profound sense of belonging. They allow us to share joys, provide support in times of adversity, and perceive the world through others' perspectives. As we move forward in this digital age, embracing these connections is critical to maintaining our human essence and preserving our societal fabric.

Despite the potential for digital technologies and AI to create a sense of isolation, we can also leverage them as tools to foster and enhance our relationships. The key lies in consciously striking a balance between utilizing technology for its benefits while ensuring that it doesn't hinder our interpersonal connections. The digital world, with its vast interconnected networks, offers numerous opportunities for connection if used thoughtfully and responsibly.

This chapter will delve into strategies and guidance for navigating human connections in a world increasingly influenced by AI and digital technology. We'll explore topics such as mindful technology use, nurturing relationships in a digital society, and leveraging technology to enhance rather than hinder our connections. We'll also delve into the realm of digital empathy—understanding and responding to the emotional needs of others through digital platforms.

By the end of this chapter, we aim to equip you with the knowledge and strategies needed to strengthen your human connections, fostering them as robust support systems that thrive alongside technology. It is a journey of learning to harness the power of technology without letting it overshadow our innate need for human interaction.

Human connections are vital for various aspects of our lives, including the following:[100]

- Emotional well-being: Strong relationships contribute to emotional well-being, providing support, validation, and a sense of belonging. Supportive relationships, which are those that involve trust, empathy, caring, and nurturing, are linked to good health, including our emotional health, because they are protective factors against stress and problems, big or small. Emotional well-being through relationships strengthens your immune system. Social disconnection, on the other hand, can make us more impulsive, more anxious, and less emotionally resilient. [100]
- Personal growth: Interacting with diverse individuals promotes personal growth, fostering empathy, understanding, and the ability to navigate complex social situations. Personal growth is also improving your own habits, behaviour, actions, and reactions. It's often said that personal growth begins when we begin to accept our own weaknesses. You can learn a lot about yourself and grow personally by interacting with other people from various backgrounds, listening to what they are saying, being open-minded to learning new things, and finding peace with things you cannot change. [101]
- Collaboration and innovation: Human connections facilitate the exchange of ideas, fostering creativity and innovation that drive progress in various fields. Innovation is not just a task reserved for a few certain people, nor does true innovation happen with just one person's ideas or work. The power of collaboration and innovation is that if we democratise innovation and involve more people, we are more likely to come up with truly innovative solutions. To encourage wider collaboration, we must push through information silos. The more people you bring in earlier in the project, the quicker you can iterate and open up information sharing. [102]
- Building trust: Face-to-face interactions and shared experiences help build trust, a crucial element in both personal and professional relationships. An important part of building trust is to show vulnerability. Part of this happens automatically over time. Building trust requires you to open yourself up to the potential of being hurt in both private and work relationships. [103]

The growing prevalence of digital technologies and AI presents both challenges and opportunities for cultivating human connections, including the following:

- Physical distance: While digital communication tools can bridge physical distances, they can also contribute to feelings of disconnection and isolation. When technology takes the place of in-person relationships, it has been found to increase loneliness and disconnection as well as reduce overall well-being. Technology can help supplement in-person relationships but should not be relied upon and a total replacement of in-person meetings. [104]
- Overreliance on technology: Relying too heavily on AI and digital tools can lead to a loss of interpersonal skills and a diminished ability to connect with others on a deeper level. A compulsion to use technology may ultimately harm users and contribute to real-life social isolation.

Having constant access to technology can prevent us from making personal connections. It has become a habit recently that in any free moment we reach for our smartphones, and this behaviour could be making our loneliness worse. [105]

- Enhanced communication: Digital technologies offer new ways to connect with others, enabling real-time communication across vast distances and providing access to diverse perspectives. Communication is instant today. Although this could be seen as a positive or a negative, as we feel always on and always connected, in the past you had to wait weeks or even months for a reply due to geographical distance. Also, social media has connected anyone and everyone. We can show our skills and creativity with the whole world on these platforms. Wireless signals, undersea cables. satellites, they all mean we receive modern communications in milliseconds. There is also the reliability factor. I'm sure we have all lost a letter or package in the post at some point in time. Yes, there is the risk of hackers when it comes to digital communications; however, most of our major technology platforms these days have end-to-end encryption. [106]
- Opportunities for collaboration: Digital platforms can facilitate collaboration among individuals and teams, fostering creativity and innovation. Technology doesn't recognise borders. We saw the entire world move online during the COVID-19 pandemic. Zoom and Teams meetings were par for the course for both work and personal situations. Technology can be a great driver in keeping connected with people who are geographically distant, and digital collaboration combines the best aspects of traditional in-person collaboration (like real-time idea exchange) and remote tools (like shared workspaces and cloud-based storage) for a truly cooperative and productive work environment. [107]

In an era where artificial intelligence is becoming increasingly ingrained in our daily lives, the need to maintain and nurture human connections has never been more pertinent. These human connections, founded on mutual respect, empathy, and understanding, form the bedrock of our collective humanity. By emphasizing meaningful interactions and fostering robust relationships, we can create a society where technology enriches rather than erodes our human connections.

Meaningful interactions stimulate emotional resonance, intellectual growth, or personal reflection. They can be as simple as a thoughtful conversation with a friend, a heartfelt gesture toward a loved one, or a collaborative project with colleagues. By consciously prioritising these types of interactions, we elevate the human experience beyond the transactional, creating bonds that are rewarding and enriching.

The role of strong relationships in preserving our humanity is also paramount. Relationships, be they familial, platonic, or professional, offer a sense of belonging and contribute to our emotional and mental well-being. In the face of AI's rapid growth, nurturing these relationships becomes vital to maintaining the human touch in our interactions and decisions.

[100] https://www.mindful.org/why-relationship-are-key-to-well-being/

[101] https://www.transcendhealth.com.au/why-is-personal-growth-important/#:~:text=Personal%20growth%20is%20the%20process,that%20they%20wish%20to%20change.

[102] https://www.washingtonpost.com/brand-studio/wp/2021/05/24/feature/how-better-collaboration-can-boost-innovation-and-success-in-the-new-normal/

[103] https://positivepsychology.com/build-trust/#:~:text=Be%20true%20to%20your%20word,you're%20unable%20to%20keep.

[104] https://www.psychologytoday.com/au/blog/live-long-and-prosper/202210/technology-use-loneliness-and-isolation

[105] https://edu.gcfglobal.org/en/thenow/is-technology-making-us-lonely/1/#

[106] https://www.techprevue.com/technology-helps-improve-communication/#:~:text=Wireless%20signals%2C%20satellites%2C%20undersea%20cables,post%20office%20or%20mail%20room.

[107] https://www.mural.co/blog/digital-collaboration#:~:text=Digital%20collaboration%20is%20the%20practice,a%20change%20in%20team%20dynamics.

Strengthening Interpersonal Relationships in the Age of AI

Maintaining our human essence amidst the rapid advancements in AI and technology is crucial. An essential part of preserving this humanity is the nurturing of interpersonal relationships. In this chapter, we will delve deeper into the importance of such relationships within the context of an increasingly AI-dominated society, and we will present practical, tangible strategies for enhancing and preserving these vital human connections.

Interpersonal relationships form the bedrock of our human experience, weaving a network of emotional support, mutual growth, and shared experiences that enrich our lives. They contribute significantly to our emotional well-being, providing us with the comfort of companionship, and the joy of shared happiness. In terms of personal growth, relationships can serve as mirrors, reflecting our strengths and areas of improvement, thereby fostering self-awareness and personal evolution. Further, they instil in us a sense of belonging, anchoring us to a community and lending a collective dimension to our individual existence.

In a world increasingly guided by AI and automation, these relationships assume even more significance. As technology pervades every facet of our lives, it is our human relationships that ground us, reminding us of our innate humanity. Therefore, as we stride into an AI-driven future, it becomes imperative to consciously nurture and strengthen our interpersonal bonds. This chapter will provide practical strategies to do so, underlining the importance of communication, empathy, shared experiences, and mutual respect in fostering and maintaining strong interpersonal relationships.

Interpersonal relationships play a critical role in our lives, contributing to our emotional well-being, personal growth, and sense of belonging. They are essential for the following:

- Emotional support: Strong relationships provide emotional support and encouragement during challenging times, promoting resilience and well-being. Emotional support is an intentional verbal or nonverbal way to show care and affection for one another. By providing emotional support, you offer people reassurance, acceptance, encouragement, and caring. Receiving emotional support helps us cope with daily problems, disappointments, or pain and makes us feel more resourceful to deal with troubles in life. [114]
- Personal development: Interacting with others helps us learn about ourselves, develop empathy and understanding, and improve our communication skills. It also helps us look inward and focus on ways to better ourselves. Personal development increases our self-awareness, self-esteem, and skills and fulfills our aspirations. Personal development is much bigger than career development, as it includes all aspects of your life. [115]

- Collaboration and innovation: Effective interpersonal relationships foster collaboration and the exchange of ideas, driving innovation and progress in various fields. Relationships drive innovation, so we want to create collaborative environments that foster innovation. Collaboration assists with more innovative solutions, quicker development time frames, and more efficient delivery. [116]
- Building trust: Positive interpersonal relationships are built on trust, which is essential for healthy personal and professional connections. Simply put, trust could be described as a situation where you are not worried about being vulnerable because you're confident that the people around you will support you and won't take advantage of your vulnerability. To build trust, consider being a good role model, be honest, be a team player, act with transparency, and avoid micromanagement. [117]
- Social cohesion: Healthy communities and support networks contribute to social cohesion, promoting shared values, cooperation, and trust. Social cohesion involves building shared values and communities of interpretation, reducing disparities in wealth and income, and generally enabling people to have a sense that they are engaged in a common enterprise, facing shared challenges, and that they are members of the same community. [118]

To create human connections in an increasingly digital world, consider the following strategies: [119]

- Prioritise face-to-face interactions: Whenever possible, prioritise in-person meetings and social gatherings over digital communication to foster deeper connections. Yes, technology is great, but face-to-face meetings remain beneficial, as they help build trust. It is said that more than 90 percent of communication is via nonverbal cues. These cues are incredibly difficult to read over video conference. In-person meetings also boost active participation. We've all had that person who joins the video conference only to continue working on their second screen, or their camera is off so they can throw a load of washing on. How engaged are these people? In-person meetings mean it's difficult for people to be anywhere else except in that moment. Face-to-face is also far more beneficial in conflict resolution. This also comes down to non-verbal cues. When you meet face-to-face you have less distraction, can be more engaged in the conversation, and work out the issue quicker and more completely. Trying to resolve conflict online can work but may not leave everyone happy with the outcome. [120]
- Set boundaries with technology: Technology is no doubt a huge part of our lives. Most of us wouldn't be able to effectively participate in employment or education or some jobs without it. We can feel entirely lost and anxious if we misplace our phones. Technical difficulties of services going down with or without warning is a trigger for some. Technology can greatly improve our learning, increase efficiency, and enhance our communication and lives. On the other hand, it can also be a huge time

waster and a big distraction. Assess your current tech use. Outside of work, how much do you use tech in your downtime? Establish boundaries for your use of technology, as too much of anything can create an imbalance and probably isn't good for us. Think about designated screen-free times or designated areas of your home where devices are not allowed. Boundaries don't have to be limiting; they can protect you from potential distractions and strengthen your relationships and personal well-being. [121]

- Participate in community activities: Engage in community-based events and activities that bring people together and provide opportunities for shared experiences and connections. Whether it's local meetups, sharing ideas in an online forum, or connecting with others in the same job role or industry, communities are everywhere, and forging these relationships is a critical part of being human. The need to be around others can have a huge psychological impact on us. It allows us to benefit from others while they benefit from us. We feel connection and a sense of duty to contribute. [122]

- Cultivate empathy and emotional intelligence: Continuously develop your emotional intelligence skills, such as empathy, self-awareness, and effective communication, to enhance your ability to connect with others. Understanding the emotional state of yourself and others is critical to any relationship private or professional. EI refers to the ability to recognise, understand, and manage your own emotions, whereas empathy is your ability to understand and share the feelings of others. Empathy allows us to connect with other people on a deeper level and to feel their emotions and respond appropriately. [123]

It is clear that fostering human connections and fortifying interpersonal relationships is of paramount importance in preserving our humanity, even as we venture deeper into the era of artificial intelligence. Our human capacity to form meaningful, emotional bonds with others, to empathize, and to engage in rich, nuanced communication sets us apart from AI and is a cornerstone of our shared human experience.

By actively prioritising and nurturing meaningful interactions, we safeguard these connections. This could mean setting digital boundaries, ensuring technology is used as a tool to augment our relationships rather than overshadow them, or embracing technology that aids in building and maintaining relationships, especially when geographical distance or circumstances may otherwise hinder communication.

Practical strategies might involve carving out tech-free zones in our daily routines, ensuring that our use of technology is mindful and intentional, or using AI as a tool to facilitate communication and strengthen connections, rather than as a replacement for personal interaction. These strategies help ensure that our relationships continue to be grounded in genuine human connection, even as our interactions become increasingly mediated by technology.

However, cultivating human connections is just one aspect of preserving our humanity in this technologically advanced era. The subsequent chapters will delve deeper into further strategies that form part of our larger goal.

In the chapters that follow, we will discuss the integral role of education and lifelong learning in fostering an informed and empathetic society capable of navigating the complexities of the AI world. We will explore the role of ethics in guiding the development and application of AI, ensuring that technology serves humanity and aligns with our shared values. Furthermore, we will examine how collaboration, both among humans and between humans and AI, can shape a future that balances the benefits and challenges of AI while also safeguarding our unique human attributes.

In summary, preserving and nurturing our human connections is essential in the digital age. Alongside this, education, ethics, and collaboration can help ensure that our future—while technologically advanced—retains its human heart. As we traverse this path, constant reflection, adaptation, and collaboration are needed to ensure a future that is enriched by technology but grounded in human values.

[114] https://www.berkeleywellbeing.com/emotional-support.html

[115] https://www.betterup.com/blog/personal-development#:~:text=Personal%20development%20is%20looking%20inward,skills%2C%20and%20fulfills%20your%20aspirations.

[116] https://www.chegg.com/homework-help/questions-and-answers/1-relationship-innovation-business-competition-innovation-creates-natural-competitiveness--q93779945

[117] https://www.mindtools.com/apb02xp/building-trust

[118] https://scanloninstitute.org.au/research/mapping-social-cohesion/what-social-cohesion

[119] https://www.betterup.com/blog/human-connection

[120] https://au.indeed.com/career-advice/career-development/face-to-face-communication#:~:text=Communicating%20face%20to%20face%20can,a%20glimpse%20into%20your%20personality.

[121] https://www.makeuseof.com/ways-to-establish-healthy-boundaries-technology/

[122] https://www.communityledgrowth.com/the-psychology-of-community-why-human-connection-makes-clg-work/

[123] https://www.linkedin.com/pulse/empathy-emotional-intelligence-understanding-patricia-pouncey/

CHAPTER 5: FOSTERING CREATIVITY AND INNOVATION

The Importance of Creativity in an AI-Driven World

In the evolving landscape of our AI-driven society, creativity and innovation have emerged as crucial traits to uphold our human uniqueness and thrive amidst rapid change. Not only does creativity distinguish us from machines, but it also propels us towards new ideas, solutions, and visions that redefine our future. As we traverse through the chapters of this book, this segment specifically emphasizes the significance of human creativity in a world increasingly influenced by artificial intelligence. Here, we will dissect the uniqueness of human creativity and its importance in an AI-dominated world and present practical strategies for nurturing and enhancing this trait in both personal and professional contexts.

Creativity, by its very nature, is inherently human. It stems from our capacity to dream, to imagine, to question, and to venture beyond the realms of logic and data-driven analysis, into a world of unrestricted potential. As AI continues to advance, it undoubtedly enhances our problem-solving capabilities, yet it falls short of replicating the originality, spontaneity, and nuanced understanding that characterizes human creativity. [124]

Within this transformative era, creativity does not merely remain an aesthetic pursuit but becomes a vital survival skill. As tasks of predictability and repetition increasingly fall within the purview of AI, our creative capacities—our ability to innovate, to connect disparate ideas, and to navigate the complexities of socio-emotional contexts—become our unique human advantage.

This chapter will offer insights into harnessing and amplifying our creative potential. We'll delve into the role of creativity in an AI-saturated world, explore the distinctive dimensions of human creativity, and shed light on its impact across multiple spheres of life. By equipping you with practical strategies, we aspire to aid you in fostering creativity in personal pursuits, professional engagements, and community endeavours.

By nurturing our creative spirit, we can maintain our human essence, even as we integrate AI into our lives. Embracing creativity allows us to steer the course of technological evolution, ensuring that we use AI as a tool for enhancing human potential rather than as a substitute for it. Join us on this journey to reclaim and celebrate the human artistry of creativity and innovation in an age deeply intertwined with artificial intelligence.

Creativity and innovation are vital for various aspects of our lives, including the following:

- Problem-solving: Creative thinking allows us to approach complex problems from unique perspectives and develop innovative solutions. This is because not all problems have straightforward solutions. The more complex a problem is, the more nuanced the solution must be. Creative problem-solving involves gathering observations, asking questions, and considering a wide range of perspectives. It encourages critical thinking, collaboration, communication, and, of course, creativity. Creative problem-solving requires you to separate your divergent and convergent thinking in order to solve problems creatively. Divergent thinking is the process of generating lots of potential solutions and possibilities (brainstorming). Convergent thinking involves reaching one well-defined solution to a problem. This type of thinking is best suited for tasks that involve logic as opposed to creativity, such as answering multiple-choice questions where you know there are no other possible solutions. [125]

- Adaptability: In a rapidly changing world, creativity fosters adaptability, enabling us to navigate new challenges and capitalize on emerging opportunities. Adaptability skills enable us to cope with and respond to change, uncertainty, and ambiguity. They require us to be flexible, resilient, creative, and open-minded. Adaptability isn't just responding to change, but it's also anticipating it and initiating it. Being adaptable is essential if we are to thrive in a rapidly changing and competitive environment. Being adaptable helps us as individuals and teams in our personal lives or in business remain relevant and competitive, manage stress and uncertainty, develop creative solutions to problems, and collaborate and communicate effectively. [126]

- Personal growth: Engaging in creative pursuits contributes to personal growth, fostering self-expression, self-awareness, and emotional well-being. Personal growth is the improvement of our skills, knowledge, wisdom, habits, behaviour, or personal qualities. Personal growth gives us the tools to thrive in a continually changing and evolving world, especially as technology impinges on our humanity. Set yourself a goal for personal growth. For example, learn to be more productive at work, get wiser with your finances, or respond with resilience to challenging circumstances. Once you have set yourself a goal, look toward the goal, design the best strategy to reach it, and focus on it. Once you have this plan, the next step is to take action, stepping out of your comfort zone and into the journey of achieving this goal. [127]

- Economic progress: Creativity and innovation drive economic growth, leading to the development of new industries, job opportunities, and improved standards of living. The creative economy describes the current and future state of the economy, where creativity and innovation are key drivers of growth. The creative economy is often viewed as a key driver of economic growth, as it can create links and spillover effects that stimulate other sectors of the economy. It can also help to diversify the economy and generate more employment opportunities. Creativity and innovation can develop new ways of delivering existing products or improving existing products or services to optimise business. There is a positive relationship between economic growth and innovation, according to the

International Monetary Fund (IMF). The evidence is clear that there are transformational effects of innovation at the macroeconomic level. Studies show that influential patents were followed by periods of high productivity growth. [128]

While AI has demonstrated remarkable capabilities in certain creative domains, human creativity possesses unique qualities that set it apart, including the following:

- Emotional depth: Human creativity is often driven by complex emotions, personal experiences, and cultural context, resulting in emotionally rich and nuanced creations. The long-standing view is that positive emotions fuel creativity because they broaden the mind, whereas negative emotions are detrimental to our creativity because they narrow our focus. This is a simplistic view but a good starting point. In actuality, both broaden your attention, and narrowing it are both key contributors to creativity. This is not something AI can do easily—at least at this point in time without being trained or further developments unlocked in the technology space to teach computers creative thinking. The current main limitation of AI is that it is unable to replicate human creativity. Machines can mimic patterns and produce work that is technically correct, but they lack the thinking and ability to imagine something that has never existed before. [129]

- Cross-disciplinary insights: Humans can draw upon diverse knowledge, experiences, and interests to generate creative ideas and solutions, transcending the limitations of domain-specific AI algorithms. The ultimate vision for AI is systems that can handle a wide range of cognitive tasks—similar to humans multi-tasking or trying to complete or work on several things at once. This vision is widely referred to as *artificial general intelligence* or AGI. For AI to be generally intelligent, it must be able to adapt as changes occur in the environment. Humans can adapt to new surroundings by drawing on past experiences, and AI must be able to do the same. [130]

- Serendipity and intuition: Human creativity often benefits from serendipitous discoveries and intuitive leaps that are difficult to replicate in AI systems. Far from the myth of the solitary genius, social interactions and even weak social ties—occasional interactions with people we are not close to—are very helpful and aid our creativity. For creative serendipity to occur, we need to expect the unexpected and be ready to take advantage of opportunities and work with the unexpected. [131] Intuition is the ability to acquire knowledge without resorting to conscious reasoning or needing explanation. This is why AI currently can't operate at a human or AGI level, because it's not conscious, cannot adapt, and does not have the experiences, emotions, or ability to make the intuitive leaps in decision-making we humans can. AI can artificially mimic some of these but cannot match human abilities in this area—yet. [132]

- Ethical considerations: Human creators can navigate ethical complexities and make value-based decisions, while AI-driven creativity may lack this moral dimension. AI may be regarded as inherently amoral, as it does not share the same fundamental principles humans adhere to, there may be human-like attributions and biases that influence the moral reasoning of AI systems. Humanity must ensure that the implications of AI are understood as much as possible and that AI is programmed and implemented in alignment with our ethical principles. [133]

To nurture creativity and innovation in an increasingly AI-driven society, consider the following strategies:

- Cultivating a growth mindset: Embrace a growth mindset that values learning, experimentation, and resilience in the face of setbacks, fostering an environment that encourages creative risk-taking.
- Encourage collaboration and diversity: Promote collaboration among diverse individuals, creating opportunities to exchange ideas and perspectives that drive innovation.
- Engage in lifelong learning: Pursue ongoing education and personal development, exploring new subjects and interests to cultivate a broad knowledge base and foster creative thinking.
- Practice deliberate creativity: Set aside time for focused creative pursuits, such as brainstorming, journaling, or artistic endeavours, to hone your creative skills and generate innovative ideas.
- Leverage technology as a creative tool: Utilise AI and digital technologies as tools to enhance, rather than replace, human creativity, capitalizing on the unique strengths of both humans and machines.

The innate human capacity for creativity sets us apart from artificial intelligence. Our ability to envision new ideas, create innovative solutions, and approach challenges from unique perspectives makes us adaptable and resilient, even in a rapidly changing, AI-driven world.

To foster and enhance this creativity, we can employ several practical strategies. Encouraging an open mindset, promoting curiosity, and embracing failure as a learning opportunity can all contribute to a thriving creative environment. Furthermore, integrating arts and culture into our everyday life, investing in continued learning and diverse experiences, and facilitating spaces for brainstorming and creative problem-solving can stimulate our imaginative capabilities.

As we progress through this book, we will delve deeper into additional strategies to maintain our humanity amid the digital revolution. These include the roles of education, ethics, and collaboration.

Education is key to understanding AI's potential and pitfalls, empowering us to make informed decisions and use AI responsibly. Emphasising ethics ensures that AI development aligns with our moral principles, resulting in technologies that respect human rights, promote fairness, and enhance societal well-being. Collaboration, on the other hand, encourages the synergistic interaction between humans and AI, leveraging the unique strengths of each to drive innovation and progress.

In sum, by nurturing our creativity and incorporating these additional strategies, we can shape a future where humans and AI coexist harmoniously, preserving our human essence while capitalizing on the benefits of AI.

[124] https://www.psychologytoday.com/au/blog/social-lights/202210/the-importance-of-creativity

[125] https://www.mindtools.com/a2j08rt/creative-problem-solving

[126] https://hbr.org/2011/07/adaptability-the-new-competitive-advantage

[127] https://blog.mindvalley.com/personal-growth/

[128] https://blog-pfm.imf.org/en/pfmblog/2022/11/effects-of-innovation-on-fiscal-policies-and-economic-growth#:~:text=There%20is%20a%20positive%20relationship,highly%20innovative%20(see%20chart).

[129] https://adpulp.com/why-artificial-intelligence-is-not-a-replacement-for-human-creativity/#:~:text=One%20of%20the%20main%20limitations,that%20has%20never%20existed%20before.

[130] https://www.techtarget.com/searchenterpriseai/feature/General-AI-vs-narrow-AI-comes-down-to-adaptability

[131] https://www.psychologytoday.com/au/blog/creativity-the-art-and-science/202106/creativity-and-serendipity-making-the-unexpected-happen

[132] https://en.wikipedia.org/wiki/Intuition

[133] https://link.springer.com/article/10.1007/s43681-022-00214-z#:~:text=While%20AI%20might%20be%20regarded,moral%20reasoning%20of%20AI%20systems.

Techniques for Enhancing Creativity and Innovation

In the face of a rapidly evolving, AI-driven society, our ability to foster creativity and innovation stands as a vital stronghold of our humanity. These attributes help us to navigate new technological landscapes, solve complex problems, and generate new ideas. This chapter will delve into an array of techniques designed to amplify creativity and spur innovation, helping individuals unlock their unique human potential and effectively synergize with the inherent strengths of AI.

Creativity is a defining trait of human intelligence. It's the process of generating original ideas that have value. In an AI-driven world, creativity has the power to inspire new solutions, broaden horizons, and introduce different perspectives that AI might not yet be able to mimic. Techniques to enhance creativity can range from setting aside dedicated brainstorming sessions to cultivating diverse environments that encourage free thinking and the exchange of ideas. [134]

Innovation, meanwhile, is the process of implementing these creative ideas into a context where they can solve a problem or meet a need. In the professional setting, fostering a culture of innovation is often crucial for organisations to stay competitive in an AI-dominated landscape. This involves creating an environment where new ideas are celebrated, learning is continuous, and the capacity for adaptive change is valued. Innovation-friendly workplaces often emphasize team collaboration, interdisciplinary approaches, and risk-taking in their culture. [135]

Brainstorming and divergent thinking techniques encourage the generation of numerous ideas and perspectives, fostering creativity and innovation. Some effective brainstorming techniques include the following:

- Freewriting or mind-mapping to generate ideas without judgement or restrictions: Mind mapping is a graphical way to represent ideas and concepts. It is a visual thinking tool that helps you structure information, notice patterns, synthesize data, recall learning, and generate new ideas. [136]
- Collaborative brainstorming sessions that encourage diverse perspectives and open dialogue: Also known as *crowd storming*, brainstorming is a way for teams or individuals from different backgrounds to come together to generate new ideas or solutions on specific topics. To really find success in collaborative brainstorming, consider the following points: Let people work alone first, as everyone takes a different approach to thinking about problems. Elevate shy voices. Some people are shy, and collaborative sessions like this can often put the shy participants at a disadvantage. Give the participants enough time to relax, understand the subject, and begin generating ideas. If you rush the focus straight to ideas, people won't come up with their best solutions. [137]
- Utilizing prompts or constraints to stimulate creative thinking and inspire unique solutions: It may seem counterintuitive, but when you're trying to push yourself creatively, constraints become quite important. They provide focus by limiting your options. Whether they are a specific prompt

to start with a structure to work within or rules for the creative process you must follow, they provide the parameters for what is fixed and what is free to explore. [138]

Cultivating a sense of curiosity and exploration can enhance creativity and innovation by broadening your knowledge base and exposing you to new ideas and perspectives. Techniques for fostering curiosity and exploration include the following:

- Pursuing new hobbies, interests, or learning opportunities: Because hobbies involve creative engagement, they encourage us to see the world from a different perspective and challenge our problem-solving skills. Creativity isn't limited to artistic hobbies. Hiking, chess, or collecting items can stimulate creative thinking, as they encourage us to strategise, recognise patterns, or see value in and beauty in unexpected places.
- Traveling or engaging in cultural experiences to gain new insights and perspectives: Creativity can also positively impact our adaptability and innovative thinking. Whilst it might sound counterintuitive, hobbies can help develop transferable skills, such as teamwork, leadership, or strategic thinking. [139]
- Actively seeking out and engaging with unfamiliar or challenging ideas and concepts.

Several problem-solving techniques can help individuals approach challenges with creativity and innovation. Some of these techniques are as follows:

- The SCAMPER method (substitute, combine, adapt, modify, put to another use, eliminate, reverse): This technique involves asking a series of questions designed to stimulate creative thinking and generate alternative solutions. There is no sequential flow to follow whilst moving through each of the seven techniques. You can use this method on an existing product, service, or idea that you want to improve, or which could be a great starting point for future development. You simply go down the list and ask questions regarding each of the seven elements, applying the questions, values, benefits, services, touch points, product attributes, pricing markets, and essentially any other related aspect that has relevance to your ideation needs. Look at the answers you came up with. Do any of them stand out as possible solutions? Could you use any of them to improve your product or develop a new product? You can then take the good ideas and explore them further. [140]

- Analogical thinking—drawing parallels between seemingly unrelated concepts or problems to inspire innovative solutions: Analogical thinking uses information from one situation, called the *base* or *source*, to deal with another situation, the *target*, that is analogous to the base. Analogies function by providing a framework for comparison across concepts, making insights easier to identify and apply—in other words, taking inspiration from what works in other industries and applying those insights to your own industry. No need to re-invent the wheel when you can replicate it in a unique way. [141]

- Design thinking: A human-centered approach to problem-solving that emphasizes empathy, experimentation, and iteration. Design thinking emphasises the importance of continuous research and evaluation and seeks input into a project from various individuals, areas, or teams within your business as a product, process, or service takes shape. Whilst various models have been developed, they all share the same basic stages: understand, explore, and materialise. At its best, design thinking is highly collaborative. It brings together people from across the organization and often from outside of it, so that a diverse group, including those whose voices are not usually heard, can participate. It centres the needs and emotions of those we hope to serve. [142]

A willingness to embrace failure and learn from mistakes is crucial for fostering creativity and innovation. Techniques for cultivating this mindset include the following:

- Reframing failure as a learning opportunity rather than a setback. It's only natural to take failure personally. Your confidence can take a hit when you make a mistake. Failure also causes stress, and when you are stressed or in a reactive mindset, you are prone to being problem focused and may lose your ability to think well. There are three steps to help reframe failure:
    - Acknowledge it, no matter its size: To productively work with failure, acknowledge it has happened. Calling something a failure takes a certain amount of courage. Over time you will become more resilient in the face of setbacks, and as a result you will get more comfortable with failure as part of any creative or innovative venture.
    - Look past failure and don't lay blame: The blame game is only likely to send you into a tailspin of anger and regret. Whilst you shouldn't be defensive, you also shouldn't blame yourself. You need the emotional distance to objectively reflect and learn from the situation.
    - Make the choice to learn from failure. What can you take accountability for? What step did you fail to take? What could you have done differently? After you have assessed the situation, be clear about what you are learning. [143]
- Encouraging experimentation and risk-taking in personal and professional settings. Both are essential for innovation and creativity. However, as outlined earlier, desired outcomes and criteria for success as well as putting in place boundaries and constraints ensure you create a supportive and stimulating environment for your team. Experimentation and risk-taking require a willingness to challenge the assumptions and

parameters that govern the situation. You must also allow the time, space, and tools to explore and test different ideas and approaches. [144]

- Analysing failures and setbacks to identify areas for growth and improvement: One of the most significant benefits of failure is the opportunity to learn and grow. Each setback provides a chance to analyse what went wrong, learn from the setback, and develop a resilient mindset. Navigating failure and setbacks by ourselves can be challenging. Seeking guidance from mentors and trusted friends can provide valuable insights and support. Failure can change your entire perspective. People who fail and bounce back have the opportunity to develop an understanding of why they failed. [145]

Our distinct human capacity for creativity, resilience in the face of failure, and our inherent curiosity serve as pillars for adaptability and endurance in a world increasingly influenced by artificial intelligence. By consciously cultivating these traits, we can not only navigate the challenges of an AI-integrated society but also tap into opportunities that such advancements offer, making our role as humans not just necessary, but irreplaceable.

Enhancing creative thinking, one of the key traits that distinguish us from machines, can be achieved through a variety of methods. Brainstorming sessions, for example, encourage the free flow of ideas and foster innovative thinking. Specialised exercises that challenge conventional thought patterns can also promote more original, out-of-the-box solutions. Furthermore, creating environments that stimulate experimentation and innovation, where new ideas are welcomed and diversity of thought is encouraged, can greatly enhance our creative capacities.

In an ever-changing world where failure is often seen as a setback, it's essential to shift our perception and instead view failure as a natural and necessary part of the learning process. By fostering a culture that sees failures as opportunities for growth and learning, we create a mindset that is not deterred by challenges but instead sees them as stepping stones to success.

Our innate curiosity, an attribute unique to humans, serves as a powerful catalyst for learning and discovery. By consciously nurturing this inquisitive nature, we keep ourselves open to new ideas and technologies, fuel our desire for knowledge, and position ourselves to continually learn and grow in tandem with the rapidly evolving AI technologies.

Through these techniques, we can ensure that our unique human attributes remain a vibrant and vital part of the AI-influenced world. By fostering creativity, embracing failure as a path to success, and stoking our curiosity, we enhance our adaptability and resilience, ensuring our meaningful co-existence with AI in the digital age.

[134] https://www.psychologytoday.com/au/blog/social-lights/202210/the-importance-of-creativity

[135] https://en.wikipedia.org/wiki/Innovation

[136] https://www.creativitywakeup.com/blog/mind-maps#:~:text=Mind%20mapping%20is%20a%20graphical,power%20lies%20in%20its%20simplicity.

[137] https://www.creativitywakeup.com/blog/mind-maps#:~:text=Mind%20mapping%20is%20a%20graphical,power%20lies%20in%20its%20simplicity.

[138] https://medium.com/ydays/how-constraints-can-inspire-creative-thinking-8a125be26091

[139] https://www.miragenews.com/more-than-just-fun-the-hidden-value-of-hobbies-1005093/

[140] https://www.designorate.com/a-guide-to-the-scamper-technique-for-creative-thinking/#google_vignette

[141] https://www.cambridge.org/core/books/abs/rethinking-creativity/analogical-thinking-in-problemsolving-and-creativity/0B0E49277F5608EEA7FBF7185C057B86

[142] https://www.smashingmagazine.com/2021/06/design-thinking-problem-solving-strategy/

[143] https://www.forbes.com/sites/dedehenley/2022/05/22/three-strategies-to-help-reframe-failure/?sh=64585eff5b48

[144] https://www.linkedin.com/advice/0/how-do-you-encourage-experimentation-risk-taking#:~:text=Experimentation%20and%20risk%2Dtaking%20require,with%20different%20methods%20and%20solutions.

[145] https://www.linkedin.com/pulse/benefits-failure-how-embrace-risk-learn-from-setbacks-ben-jamin-toy/

The Role of Arts, Culture, and Humanities in Maintaining Human Identity

The increasing importance of arts, culture, and humanities cannot be understated. These disciplines provide us with critical anchors to our humanity, nurturing creativity and innovation and fostering a profound sense of connection. This chapter aims to illuminate the significance of arts, culture, and humanities in our increasingly digitized society, and how they can help us thrive alongside AI.

The arts, which encompass visual art, literature, music, theatre, and more, have long served as expressions of human creativity and emotion. They encapsulate our ability to think abstractly, empathise, and communicate complex ideas and feelings—capabilities that set us apart from AI. In the age of AI, the arts can provide a counterbalance to technology's quantitative bias, emphasising the qualitative, subjective, and uniquely human. They can also inspire innovation, as the freedom of artistic expression often leads to novel ideas and perspectives that can be translated across disciplines.

Culture, a system of shared beliefs, values, customs, behaviours, and artifacts, plays a vital role in shaping our identity and societal structures. It forms the bedrock of our collective history and helps us make sense of the world. In the context of AI, culture serves as a reminder of our shared human experience, ensuring that technological advances are grounded in a broader understanding of human values, norms, and societal needs. Moreover, culture shapes our interpretation and application of AI, influencing how we integrate it into our lives and workplaces.

Humanities, the study of human society and culture, encourages critical thinking, empathy, and a deep understanding of the human condition. Disciplines such as philosophy, literature, history, sociology, and others provide the tools to question, analyse, and interpret the world around us. As AI continues to permeate our lives, the humanities can guide us in navigating the ethical, social, and political implications of these technologies. They can help us design and use AI in a way that respects human dignity, values, and rights.

By integrating arts, culture, and humanities into our daily lives and technological innovations, we can foster a society that not only uses AI but also understands and critically engages with it. In a world where AI can calculate, predict, and optimize, arts, culture, and humanities remind us of the importance of questioning, interpreting, and empathising. They encourage us to draw on our unique human strengths and capabilities, ensuring that we do not just survive but thrive in an AI-driven society. This chapter will further delve into the tangible ways these disciplines can be woven into our individual lives, communities, and interaction with AI.

Arts, culture, and humanities play a crucial role in our lives, [146] contributing to the following:

- Self-expression and emotional well-being: Engaging in artistic and cultural pursuits allows individuals to express themselves and explore their emotions, fostering emotional well-being and self-awareness. Self-expression in the arts positively affects mood, function, cognition, and behaviour. Self-expression plays a significant role in developing our ability to relate to others and engage in deep relationships. [147]
- Empathy and understanding: Exposure to diverse cultural and artistic expressions promotes empathy and understanding among individuals, fostering tolerance and appreciation for different perspectives. Art can be a powerful way for us to gain a better understanding of human emotions and stories. It gives us a unique lens to look at artists' inner worlds. It trains our brains to slow down and think more rationally, instead of emotionally. It restores our capacity to connect with others. Art plays a unique role in re-establishing humanity in this technology-dominated world. [148]
- Cultural preservation and identity: Arts, culture, and humanities serve as vehicles for preserving and sharing cultural heritage, promoting a sense of identity and belonging within communities. The importance of any kind of art to society and culture is unending. Art, in its varied forms, preserves the culture of people, and it does so using different forms of expression and touching on different aspects of preservation. Performing art forms and skills associated with traditional craftsmanship are significant in terms of maintaining cultural diversity in the face of growing globalisation. Promoting these art forms leads to an understanding of the intangible cultural heritage of different communities, which in turn stirs up mutual respect for each other's ways of life. [149]
- Critical thinking and problem-solving: The study of humanities encourages critical thinking, analysis, and interpretation, fostering the development of essential problem-solving skills. *Problem-solving* and *critical thinking* refer to the ability to use knowledge, facts, and data to effectively solve problems. This doesn't mean you need to have an immediate answer; it means you have to be able to think on your feet, assess problems, and find solutions. The arts and humanities teach us who we are and what we can be. They lie at the very core of the culture of which we're a part. Humanities expand our knowledge of human cultures and help us understand what binds us together and what differentiates us from one another. In addition to these high-level insights, however, they also provide practical applications that can enhance your professional skill set and give you a competitive edge. [150]

To cultivate creativity and innovation and maintain our human identity in an AI-driven world, it is essential to integrate arts, culture, and humanities into our daily lives. Some strategies for achieving this integration include the following:

- Encouraging artistic and cultural pursuits: Provide opportunities for individuals to engage in artistic and cultural activities, such as painting, writing, dancing, or attending cultural events.
- Incorporating arts and humanities in education: Advocate for the inclusion of arts, culture, and humanities in educational curricula, emphasizing the value of these disciplines in fostering creativity, critical thinking, and emotional well-being.
- Supporting artists and cultural institutions: Financially and emotionally support artists, cultural institutions, and organisations that preserve and promote cultural heritage, ensuring their continued existence and relevance in an AI-driven society.

While AI may at times seem at odds with human-centered disciplines like the arts, culture, and humanities, there is potential for productive collaboration and mutual enrichment. Some opportunities for integrating AI and human creativity include the following:

- AI-assisted creativity: Utilise AI tools and technologies to enhance human creativity, leveraging AI algorithms to generate new ideas, refine artistic techniques, or collaborate on creative projects. Co-creation between humans and AI is becoming increasingly prevalent as artists, musicians, writers, and designers collaborate with AI to produce innovative works. For example, Google's Magenta project utilises AI to generate music and visual art in collaboration with human artists. These examples highlight the growing synergy between human creativity and AI capabilities. AI is not only capable of generating creative content on its own but also of enhancing human creativity by offering new perspectives, ideas, and inspiration. [151]
- Ethical considerations and AI in the arts: Engage in discussions surrounding the ethical implications of AI in the arts, such as questions of authorship, authenticity, and intellectual property. As AI-assisted creativity becomes more sophisticated, ethical considerations surrounding authenticity, intellectual property, and originality have emerged. Questions arise about how AI-generated works can be considered original or authentic and whether AI should be credited as a co-creator alongside humans. Intellectual property rights and fair compensation for AI-generated content also pose significant challenges. [152]
- Exploring AI through arts and humanities: Use artistic and cultural expressions to explore and discuss the impact of AI on society, fostering critical thinking and dialogue about the role of AI in our lives.

It is apparent that the arts, culture, and humanities hold a pivotal role in maintaining our unique human identity amidst the technological advancements driven by artificial intelligence. These disciplines, embodying the core of our shared human experience, provide a nurturing ground for creativity and innovation that AI, as of yet, cannot replicate.

By embedding the arts, culture, and humanities into our everyday lives, we create a space for emotional expression, critical thinking, and personal growth. These disciplines challenge our perspectives, provoke thoughtful conversations, and encourage us to view the world through various lenses. This in turn promotes creativity and innovation, characteristics that are not only distinctively human but also essential for our survival and success in a rapidly changing society.

Moreover, exploring the possibilities for collaboration between AI and human creativity presents an exciting frontier. From creating new forms of art using AI to leveraging machine learning for uncovering cultural insights, the integration of technology and creativity can lead to unprecedented possibilities. Such a fusion not only enhances our creative potential but also serves as a constant reminder of our human capacity for imagination, something that stands distinct from the capabilities of AI. [153]

However, engagement with arts, culture, and humanities is only one aspect of preserving our humanity in the age of AI. The forthcoming chapters will delve into more strategies that contribute to our larger goal of maintaining our humanity in a world increasingly influenced by AI.

We will discuss the importance of education in cultivating an informed and empathetic society that is prepared to navigate the ethical challenges presented by AI. We will also explore the role of ethics in AI development and deployment, ensuring that technology serves human needs and values. Furthermore, we will examine how collaboration—among humans and between humans and AI—can shape a harmonious future where AI augments our capabilities rather than threatening our human essence.

In sum, embracing the arts, culture, and humanities is crucial in a world where technology is rapidly redefining our lives. These disciplines, along with education, ethics, and collaboration, can help us maintain our unique human qualities and thrive in an AI-driven society. As we navigate this journey, it is essential to continually reflect, adapt, and collaborate to ensure a future that is both technologically advanced and rich in human values.

[146] https://www.eden-gallery.com/news/why-is-art-important#:~:text=Art%20%26%20Its%20Role%20in%20Society&text=It%20helps%20us%20understand%20what,self%2Dreflection%20or%20social%20influence.

[147] https://www.drawchange.org/post/selfexpression#:~:text=Art%20gives%20us%20the%20ability,function%2C%20cognition%2C%20and%20behavior.

[148] https://new.artsmia.org/stories/art-and-empathy-four-thought-leaders-explain-the-connection

[149] https://www.prazzlemagazine.com/post/why-art-as-an-important-tool-for-cultural-preservation#:~:text=One%20of%20the%20ways%20art,available%20for%20people%20to%20use.

[150] https://insight.study.csu.edu.au/why-study-humanities/

[151] https://www.linkedin.com/pulse/evolution-ai-assisted-creativity-from-algorithmic-inspiration-bron/

[152] https://www.linkedin.com/pulse/ai-arts-how-technology-enhancing-creativity-tal-navarro/

[153] https://www.bbvaopenmind.com/en/articles/artificial-intelligence-and-the-arts-toward-computational-creativity/

CHAPTER 6: LIFELONG LEARNING AND ADAPTABILITY

The Necessity of Continuous Learning

The tenets of lifelong learning and adaptability become increasingly paramount for upholding our humanity and prospering amidst the whirlwind of change. AI, though a game-changer in numerous ways, makes the landscape of knowledge and skills highly fluid. To navigate this fluidity, adopting a mindset that embraces constant learning and adaptability is essential. In this chapter, we delve into the importance of these traits and provide strategies and practical guidance for fostering a growth mindset, embracing the ethos of lifelong learning, and promoting adaptability in an AI-dominated society.

Lifelong learning, as the term suggests, is the ongoing, voluntary pursuit of knowledge for personal or professional reasons. This continuous quest to learn and adapt helps us remain relevant, resilient, and ready to take on the challenges and opportunities ushered in by AI. It also reaffirms our humanity, emphasizing the uniquely human thirst for knowledge, curiosity, and progress. [154]

Adaptability, on the other hand, refers to our ability to adjust to new conditions, a trait that's highly valued in this age of rapid technological advancement. By embracing adaptability, we not only equip ourselves to survive in an evolving world, but also to thrive, seizing new opportunities that arise with the changes.

This chapter offers a deep dive into these indispensable skills of the future. We will examine why lifelong learning and adaptability are key for individuals and societies navigating the AI revolution. We will also share strategies for fostering a growth mindset, a foundational attitude that underlies the pursuit of lifelong learning and adaptability. From exploring different learning modalities to providing practical guidance on how to cultivate resilience and adaptability, this chapter serves as a comprehensive guide to thriving in our AI-integrated world.

As we continue to interact with AI, it's essential to keep learning, growing, and adapting. Embracing lifelong learning and adaptability not only helps us stay ahead of the curve but also enhances our human potential and enriches our experiences. Join us in this chapter as we chart a course towards a future where humans and AI coexist harmoniously, underpinned by the principle of lifelong learning and the spirit of adaptability.

Continuous learning and adaptability are essential for various reasons, including the following:

- Keeping pace with technological advancements: As AI and other technologies continue to evolve, individuals must adapt and acquire new skills to remain relevant and competitive in the job market. As we have seen with the rapid progress in the field of AI and even other technology, the tech industry is constantly evolving, and we must be willing to adapt to new technologies and ideas to stay relevant and succeed in our careers. This is applicable to just about any field, but in the technology industry, innovation and creativity are highly valued. If you are a software developer, you can't just learn one coding language and then be done with it. There are constant developments and new products we need to keep up with. By learning new skills and being adaptive, we can develop new and innovative ideas that lead to better or new products and services. New technologies always inevitably disrupt the industry, and those who are not prepared to adapt may find themselves being left behind. By being proactive and identifying or at least being aware of incoming changes, you position yourself as proactive rather than reactive in the face of change. [155]

- Fostering personal growth and development: Lifelong learning contributes to personal growth, fostering self-awareness, creativity, and emotional well-being. Personal growth has a direct relationship with self-discovery and life-long learning. In personal growth, leaders must participate in activities that stretch their boundaries. Simple activities are not enough to complete the development; one must also reflect on behaviours, personal values, and desires. [156]

- Enhancing problem-solving and critical thinking skills: Continuous learning and adaptability enable individuals to approach challenges with flexibility, critical thinking, and innovative problem-solving skills. Problem-solving and critical thinking are ways of systematically and objectively judging information and arguments. We can find solutions to problems by analysing and putting together data from different sources. Critical thinkers can identify new ideas and opportunities that others may have overlooked by approaching challenges with a fresh perspective. You learn different perspectives through your lifelong learning journey. Being able to approach problems from different points of view and be adaptable in the face of change and being able to pivot and stay flexible to embrace new ideas and ways of thinking will often result in better solutions to roadblocks. [157]

- Strengthening social connections: Engaging in lifelong learning can promote social connections and collaboration, fostering a sense of belonging and community. Lifelong learning can be a social event because so much of our learning comes from those we surround ourselves with. The desire to learn can encourage people to seek out relationships with those who may be able to teach you a new skill or connect with people who have a shared interest. Continuous learning often takes the form of active community engagement, where you are working with other students, people in your community, or even people in your office. [158]

To cultivate adaptability and embrace lifelong learning in an AI-driven society, consider the following strategies:

- Develop a growth mindset: Cultivate a mindset that values learning, experimentation, and resilience in the face of setbacks. Embrace challenges as opportunities for growth and improvement. Essentially, a growth mindset is a belief talent can be developed rather than regarding it as an innate gift. A person with a growth mindset puts effort and resources into learning and developing, whereas a person with a fixed mindset may not value learning and development as highly. Although elements of both exist in all of us, everyone is actually a mix of fixed and growth mindsets, and that mix continually evolves over time. A common misconception about a growth mindset is that it places value only on effort, without regard for results. Efforts matter; they are how we learn and grow. However, outcomes matter just as much. Rewarding progress and valuing processes lead to improved outcomes. [159]
- Engage in continuous learning: We can sit around all day and think, "I'll start tomorrow", or come up with excuses as to why we shouldn't take that course or read that book. We have to make a choice to pursue ongoing education and personal development through formal courses, online platforms, workshops, or self-directed learning opportunities. Diversify your learning experiences to develop a broad range of skills and knowledge.
- Leverage technology as a learning tool: Utilise AI and digital technologies to enhance your learning experiences, accessing personalised resources and leveraging online platforms for skill development and knowledge acquisition. Technology can help learners get more out of traditional instruction by providing them opportunities to implement what they learn right then and there. There is no single educational tech initiative or platform that will achieve the same results everywhere, simply because everyone learns in different ways. Find the platform that works for you, whether it's YouTube channels, online step-by-step guides, or short courses on platforms like Khan Academy or Coursera. [160]

To successfully integrate lifelong learning into your daily routine, consider the following practical tips:

- Set clear learning goals: Identify specific learning objectives that align with your personal and professional aspirations. Establish short-term and long-term goals to guide your learning journey. When learning goals are explicitly stated and shared, they help us set our own learning expectations. You will enter your training with a clearer understanding of what you expect to learn and get out of the course. [161]
- Allocate dedicated time for learning: Schedule regular time for learning activities, ensuring that you prioritise personal and professional development amid your daily responsibilities. There are two types of learning: dedicated learning time and learning in the flow of work.

Dedicated learning time is where time is specifically set aside for learning. It generally involves virtual, hybrid, or in-person training curated by a provider. The second is learning in the flow of work. This describes learning opportunities that are integrated into your workday, whether it's microlearning to figure out a skill quickly or using a search engine to understand a business term. People and employees who spend time learning at work are less likely to feel stressed and more likely to feel productive and successful. [162]

- Reflect on your learning experiences: Engage in regular reflection to assess your progress, identify areas for improvement, and celebrate your achievements. Use your reflections to inform your ongoing learning journey and adjust your goals as needed. When you reflect on your learning journey, you become aware of the skills you have developed and the skills that require more refining or that you wish to develop further. Reflective learning allows learners to step back from the experience, helping them to develop critical thinking skills and improve future performance by analysing what they have accomplished and how far they have come. [163]

- Stay curious and open-minded: Approach new experiences and ideas with curiosity and an open mind, seeking opportunities for learning and growth in both familiar and unfamiliar situations. Open-mindedness and curiosity are essential for true learning and personal growth. These traits help us challenge our existing beliefs and assumptions whilst leading us to greater self-awareness and intellectual development. [164]

In summation, the significance of lifelong learning and adaptability cannot be overstated when it comes to preserving our human essence and thriving amidst the increasing pervasiveness of artificial intelligence. It is through the continuous pursuit of knowledge, the cultivation of a mindset centred on growth, and the astute utilization of AI and other digital technologies as tools for learning that we ensure our resilience and adaptability, enabling us to adeptly navigate the multifaceted challenges that the future holds.

The concept of lifelong learning underscores the importance of continuous education and self-improvement, beyond the traditional confines of formal education. In an AI-driven world where the speed of technological advancements can render certain skills obsolete almost overnight, the commitment to continuous learning allows us to stay relevant, competitive, and capable of contributing to our rapidly evolving societies.

Similarly, cultivating a growth mindset—an attitude that embraces challenges, persists in the face of setbacks, sees effort as a path to mastery, learns from criticism, and finds lessons and inspiration in the success of others—is pivotal. Such a mindset not only equips us to better deal with the rapid changes brought about by AI but also enables us to see these changes not as threats, but as opportunities for growth and development.

Moreover, leveraging AI and digital technologies as tools for learning affords us the chance to enhance our knowledge and skills in ways previously unimagined. With the help of these technologies, we can access a wealth of information, learn at our own pace, customize our learning experiences, and even gain insights into our own learning processes.

Looking ahead, as we continue to explore the coexistence of humans and AI in the digital age, we will delve into additional strategies for preserving our human identity and values. We will examine the critical role of education, not merely as a stage in life, but as a lifelong endeavour. We will discuss ethics as it pertains to AI development and deployment, ensuring that AI technologies align with our societal values and principles. Furthermore, we will delve into the importance of collaboration—among humans and between humans and AI—in shaping a harmonious future where technology serves as a tool for human advancement, not a replacement for human roles.

[154] https://www.valamis.com/hub/lifelong-learning#:~:text=Lifelong%20learning%20is%20a%20form,school%2C%20university%20or%20corporate%20training.

[155] https://www.techtalent.co.uk/post/the-importance-of-continuous-learning

[156] https://journalofleadershiped.org/jole_articles/developing-life-long-learners-through-personal-growth-projects/

[157] https://www.linkedin.com/pulse/critical-thinking-key-lifelong-learning-personal-growth-aguimar-neto

[158] https://blog.kao.kendal.org/the-social-benefits-of-lifelong-learning

[159] https://www.linkedin.com/pulse/embracing-growth-mindset-through-continuous-learning-training-ray/

[160] https://www.brookings.edu/articles/realizing-the-promise-how-can-education-technology-improve-learning-for-all/

[161] https://iopn.library.illinois.edu/pressbooks/instructioninlibraries/chapter/establishing-learning-goals-and-outcomes/#:~:text=When%20learning%20goals%20are%20explicitly,an%20appropriate%20level%20for%20them.

[162] https://www.linkedin.com/business/talent/blog/learning-and-development/how-to-help-employees-make-time-for-learning-at-work

[163] https://learningpool.com/why-reflection-encourages-a-better-learning-experience/#:~:text=Reflective%20learning%20is%20a%20way,how%20far%20they%20have%20come.

[164] https://www.linkedin.com/pulse/power-open-mindedness-curiosity-stimulating-eng-mauricio-s%C3%A1nchez/

Developing a Growth Mindset

The advent of artificial intelligence and the rapid pace of technological change have made adaptability and continuous learning vital skills for the modern world. These abilities, strongly tied to a growth mindset, are the subject of exploration in this chapter, as they play a central role in our ability to thrive in an AI-driven society.

A *growth mindset*, conceptualized by psychologist Carol Dweck, [165] is characterized by the belief that abilities, intelligence, and talents can be developed through dedication, effort, and continuous learning. It contrasts with a *fixed mindset*, where individuals believe their abilities are set and unchangeable. The difference between these mindsets is not just a matter of outlook; it translates into significant differences in behaviour, goals, and the ability to cope with challenges.

Cultivating a growth mindset is not just a positive personal development strategy; it's a necessity in an age where technology and AI are transforming the way we live and work. By understanding and embracing the principles of a growth mindset, we can foster a society that is resilient, innovative, and fully equipped to harness the opportunities of the AI-driven future. The insights and strategies provided in this chapter will serve as a guide for individuals, educators, leaders, and organisations seeking to cultivate this essential mindset.

A growth mindset is essential for thriving in an AI-driven world for several reasons:

- Resilience and adaptability: A growth mindset fosters resilience and adaptability by encouraging people to see failures as opportunities for growth rather than insurmountable setbacks. *Resilience* is the quality that allows people to be knocked down or stumble on a roadblock but come back and overcome these obstacles stronger than before. Resilient individuals don't wallow in or dwell on failures; they acknowledge the situation, learn from their mistakes, and move forward. Resilience is vital, as the world of work is littered with challenges: difficult bosses, competitive colleagues, and tight deadlines, etc. Resilient individuals can navigate these trials, learning and growing from each experience. *Adaptability* is the ability to change or adjust in response to new conditions. In a career context, it can mean being open to new ideas or changes in the job market or your particular industry. It's about being flexible and willing to modify your behaviour, strategies, and actions to achieve your goals. In an AI-driven world where change is constant, this outlook enables individuals to adapt, learn new skills, and remain relevant and effective. [166]
- Creativity and innovation: With a growth mindset, creativity flourishes as individuals are more willing to take risks, experiment, and explore new ideas. They're not held back by the fear of failure, fostering an environment where innovation thrives—a crucial quality in today's fast-paced technological landscape. People with a fixed mindset tend to retain the same beliefs, have the same thoughts, and follow the same routines.

They only value outcomes. If the outcome isn't successful, they view the entire project as a waste. A person with a growth mindset is empowered by the belief that they can change. They see that effort can result in change for the better, and this provides them with motivation. They motivate themselves and others and add value to the overall cause. [167]

- Enhancing personal and professional relationships: A growth mindset supports effective communication, collaboration, and empathy, strengthening interpersonal relationships in both personal and professional settings. It can enhance collaboration by creating an environment where feedback is welcomed, diverse perspectives are valued, and team members are encouraged to learn from each other.

To develop a growth mindset and embrace lifelong learning and adaptability, consider the following strategies:

- Reframe challenges as opportunities: View challenges and setbacks as opportunities for growth and learning rather than insurmountable obstacles. Embrace uncertainty and change as catalysts for personal development. When things go wrong, try to reframe them in new, more positive contexts and turn them into opportunities to be taken advantage of rather than problems to avoid. [168]
- Value effort and progress over perfection: Focus on the process of learning and the effort involved, rather than solely on the end results. Celebrate progress and small victories, recognising that growth often occurs incrementally. Don't let perfection be the enemy of progress or productivity. In today's fast-paced, very public world, we are increasingly caught up in analysis paralysis when it comes to the content we are publishing or sharing. It's easy to understand why though: a never-ending news cycle and sometimes hostile social media landscape can put a magnifying glass on your work, and judgement is only ever a few clicks away. Striving for perfection is admirable, but perfect is totally subjective and varies based on each person's understanding and expectations. [169]
- Embrace failure as a learning opportunity: Rather than fearing failure or avoiding risks, view mistakes as valuable learning experiences that can inform future growth and development. Embracing failure runs counter to our most base survival instincts and the very basis on which most businesses reward the behaviour of their people. People who haven't failed have had fewer occasions on which to look deeply into themselves and understand their motivations. In failing, you learn why the things you were ignoring were actually important. [170]
- Seek and embrace constructive feedback: Actively seek feedback from others and view it as an opportunity for growth and improvement. Be open to critique and willing to adjust your approach based on the insights you receive. If you want to apply a growth mindset to your relationships, consider adopting a positive and optimistic attitude. Believe that you and others can change and improve and that relationships can get better over

time. Ask for and accept honest and respectful feedback from others, using it to learn and grow rather than feel offended or discouraged. [171]

The essential role of a growth mindset in embracing lifelong learning and adaptability is increasingly clear. In a world that is continually reshaped by advancements in artificial intelligence, developing a growth mindset—a state of mind that embraces challenges, perseveres in the face of setbacks, and sees effort as the pathway to mastery—is not just beneficial, but a necessity.

A growth mindset sets the foundation for continuous learning and adaptation. It emboldens us to step out of our comfort zones, to be resilient amid change, and to view failures not as the end but as part of the learning process. This perspective is particularly critical in our present AI-driven world, where the only constant is change, and the ability to learn, unlearn, and relearn becomes the key to staying relevant.

Fostering a growth mindset is more than just personal development—it also significantly influences how we navigate the landscape of opportunities and challenges presented by AI. It encourages curiosity and critical thinking, equipping us to ask the right questions about how AI can be used responsibly and ethically. It supports resilience, enabling us to navigate the uncertainty and disruption that AI advancements can bring. Most importantly, it promotes a love for continuous learning—a trait that's vital in a world where AI continues to redefine the boundaries of what is possible.

However, developing a growth mindset is just one piece of the puzzle. In the subsequent chapters, we will dive into further strategies that contribute to maintaining our humanity in the digital age. We will delve into the role of education, not merely as a system for imparting knowledge but as a tool for cultivating a deep sense of empathy, ethics, and social responsibility. We will explore the importance of ethical considerations in shaping AI's development and deployment, ensuring it serves to enhance humanity rather than detract from it. Furthermore, we will unpack the significance of collaboration in driving harmonious coexistence between humans and AI, underscoring the value of human connection and mutual understanding.

The journey towards preserving our humanity in the age of AI is one filled with promise and challenges. It requires a collective commitment to growth, resilience, and continuous learning. As we move forward, let's remember to nurture our uniquely human qualities, such as empathy, creativity, and a growth mindset, as these will help us thrive in a world increasingly driven by artificial intelligence.

[165] https://www.mindtools.com/asbakxx/dwecks-fixed-and-growth-mindsets

[166] https://www.creativetaxrecruitment.com/blog/2023/05/the-power-of-resilience-and-adaptability-navigating-career-challenges-for-long-term-success?source=google.com

[167] https://fortitudebusinessconsulting.com.au/why-mindset-matters-to-innovation/

[168] https://vidaaventura.net/reframing-how-to-turn-problems-into-opportunities/

[169] https://golaunchtech.com/blog/dont-let-perfection-get-in-the-way-of-progress/#:~:text=%E2%80%9CPerfection%20is%20the%20enemy%20of,to%20proceed%20on%20a%20project.

[170] https://www.startupgrind.com/blog/6-reasons-why-you-should-embrace-failure/

[171] https://www.linkedin.com/advice/0/how-do-you-cultivate-curiosity-openness-your#:~:text=If%20you%20want%20to%20cultivate,Second%2C%20embrace%20feedback%20and%20criticism.

Strategies for Upskilling and Reskilling in the Age of AI

In an AI-driven world, workforce dynamics are in a constant state of flux. Automation and technological advancements are reshaping industries, rendering some roles obsolete, and birthing new ones. In this ever-changing landscape, the concepts of upskilling and reskilling become central to individual competitiveness and career growth. As the importance of learning new skills (upskilling) and acquiring new competencies to transition into different roles (reskilling) increases, the need for clear guidance and strategies becomes paramount.

The impact of upskilling and reskilling reaches beyond the individual. It has profound implications for adaptation to technological change, career progression, and even broader economic competitiveness. Organisations, educational institutions, and governments are recognising this transformation, providing various platforms and resources to support continuous learning.

Adapting to the evolving demands of one's job or industry through upskilling requires a deep understanding of personal strengths, weaknesses, and interests and an eye on the industry's shifting needs. Individuals must be proactive in creating targeted learning plans, utilizing online platforms, engaging in workshops and bootcamps, and collaborating with employers to identify opportunities for internal training and development. Networking and community engagement further foster collaboration and support, while consideration of time, resources, and alignment with industry trends remains crucial.

Reskilling presents a pathway to navigate changes in the job market or industry trends. The ability to transition into different roles by acquiring new competencies keeps individuals relevant and adaptable, contributing to personal growth and economic agility.

This chapter will explore various strategies for upskilling and reskilling in the age of AI, providing practical guidance for continuous professional development and career growth. By actively investing in these lifelong learning strategies, individuals can maintain their relevance, resilience, and capability to thrive in a technologically advanced landscape.

Upskilling and reskilling are essential in the age of AI for several reasons:

- Adaptability in a changing job market: As AI transform industries and displaces certain jobs, upskilling and reskilling enable individuals to adapt to new roles and responsibilities, minimising the risk of unemployment. The rise of AI has brought about a significant shift in the job market. Jobs that were once thought of as secure are now at risk of being lost to AI and automation. However, even in the face of job displacement, AI and technology evolution is creating new opportunities and jobs which require specialised skills and expertise. Changing with the job market is important to stay relevant, take advantage of new possibilities, and make yourself more employable. In today's world, where things change quickly, being flexible helps you keep your job on track by keeping up with new trends and technological advances. It helps you deal with economic uncertainty and gives you access to new opportunities. [172]

- Enhanced employability and career growth: Acquiring new skills and competencies increases employability and opens up new career opportunities, fostering professional growth and development. New learning also creates motivation and engagement at work, fulfilling our essential need to grow and develop throughout our working lives. It's also relevant if you are feeling stagnant in your current career or reconsidering your career path. The modern world is data driven, and with the explosion in technologies such as AI, technology-based skills are important. The more knowledge you have in this area, the better you become at being able to pivot or find work in new fields. [173]

- Meeting the demand for AI-related skills: The rapid advancement of AI technologies creates a growing demand for professionals with AI-related skills, making upskilling and reskilling essential for staying relevant in the job market. Because AI encompasses a broad range of technologies and subfields, employers are looking for workers with different specific skill sets that fall under the AI umbrella based on their individual use cases. Some of the skills required across the field of AI include machine learning, natural language processing, neural networks, autonomous driving, visual image recognition, and robotics. A typical misconception about AI is that it will render countless jobs obsolete. I believe it will have the opposite effect. This technology will simply take over the dull and repetitive tasks within those jobs at so-called risk. As countless industries race to implement AI, there is a great opportunity to upskill or reskill to take advantage of the changing job market. [174]

To effectively upskill and reskill in an AI-driven society, consider the following strategies:

- Identify in-demand skills: Research the skills and competencies that are most in demand in your industry or the job market. Prioritise acquiring skills that align with your career goals and enhance your employability. It's been predicted that 85 percent of the jobs that will be available in 2030 don't exist at the time of writing this book (2023). Factors including the shift to remote working, emergence of the gig economy, and increasing expectations of flexibility from employers will play a part in changing which skills become in demand. I don't believe that AI will make humans redundant. AI will displace humans in repetitive and mundane tasks, which isn't really anything new, as it's been happening as long as we have tried to automate tasks, workflows, and processes. Many new roles will be created and opened up to humans as technology advances. These new roles will centre around fields that involve uniquely human skills that machines or technology simply can't replicate, skills such as creativity, human-to-human communication, emotional intelligence, and complex decision-making. We have already outlined a lot of these skills and their importance in this book. [175]

- Leverage online learning platforms: Utilise online learning platforms, such as massive open online courses (MOOCs), webinars, and e-learning courses, to acquire new skills and competencies at your own pace and on your own schedule. Online learning is a powerful way to advance your skills, so how do you make the most of these opportunities? The first step is to identify your learning needs and goals. What skills, knowledge, or credentials do you want to acquire or improve? How do they align with your aspirations and interests? Once you know this, you can then search with a better idea for courses or programs that will match your criteria and offer maximum return on investment. The second step is to find quality content. In the internet age, there are so many online learning resources and platforms, from free to paid and self-led to instructor-led. Consider factors such as the course content, instructor experience or credentials, and previous learner feedback. Also be sure to understand the time commitment, assessment methods, and support available throughout the course. [176]

- Pursue certifications and credentials: Obtain industry-recognised certifications and credentials to demonstrate your expertise in a specific skill set, enhancing your professional credibility and marketability. Personally, I do love free online courses once I've researched them based on the steps above. However, certification publicly demonstrates your commitment to continued learning and helps boost your professional credibility. The benefits of certification-based learning include increased marketability, increased earning power, improved reputation, validation of knowledge, and respect from peers. [177]

- Engage in hands-on learning experiences: Complement your theoretical knowledge with practical, hands-on learning experiences, such as internships, apprenticeships, or volunteer work, to develop your skills in real-world contexts. These real-world contexts and learning by doing mean you can work through challenges you may encounter in the real world in a safe environment and develop your problem-solving skills. Practice makes perfect, too, so incorporating hands-on learning into your study means you can refine your skills through repetition. Further, hands-on learning means you get the opportunity for instant feedback, instruction, and critique. You can benefit from interactions with other students and the instructors straight away as you learn your skills. [178]

To maximize the effectiveness of your upskilling and reskilling efforts, consider the following practical tips:

- Set SMART goals: [179] Establish specific, measurable, achievable, relevant, and time-bound (SMART) goals for your upskilling and reskilling efforts, providing clear benchmarks and timelines for your professional development. Let's break down each parameter:

- S: Specific. What needs to be accomplished/who's responsible for it? What steps need to be taken to achieve it?
- M: Measurable. This is where you should incorporate measurable, trackable benchmarks.
- A: Achievable. Goals should be realistic, so ask yourself whether your objective is something you or your team can reasonably accomplish.
- R: Relevant. You need to think about the bigger picture. Why are you setting the goal you are setting?
- T: Time-bound. To really measure success, you need to know when a goal has been reached. What's your time horizon? When will you start creating and implementing the tasks you have identified? When will you finish?

- Allocate dedicated time for learning: Schedule regular time for upskilling and reskilling activities, ensuring that you prioritise professional development amid your daily responsibilities. At the most fundamental level, we are a neotenic species, born with an instinct to learn throughout our lives. So it makes sense that we are constantly looking for ways to do things better. However, sometimes the urgency of work invariably trumps the luxury of learning. Scheduling dedicated time for learning and blocking it out in your calendar gives it a sense of importance, like a meeting you wouldn't miss. It also lets your colleagues or those around you know how important learning is to you. [180]
- Continuously reassess your progress and goals: Regularly assess your progress towards your upskilling and reskilling goals, adjusting your learning strategy as needed to align with your evolving career aspirations and industry trends. Goal setting requires intentional thinking and awareness about your current trajectory. Revisit your *why*. Why did you set this goal? Why is it important to you? It's OK to make choices that move you away from your goal as long as you recognise you are making a choice. Continuously consider the bigger picture. Most of the time people set goals simply due to the path they are on. Does this goal still make sense in the larger context? [181]

As we conclude this chapter, the importance of upskilling and reskilling as powerful tools for fostering professional growth in the evolving AI landscape becomes ever more apparent. In this rapidly changing world, where AI technologies continue to redefine traditional job roles and create new career avenues, continuous learning and professional development are no longer just options; they are vital for our professional survival and advancement.

The dynamic nature of today's job market, influenced significantly by the advent of AI, calls for individuals to be adaptable, resourceful, and committed to learning. Upskilling, which involves learning new skills within one's field, and reskilling, which entails acquiring skills for a new job role, are strategies that empower individuals to navigate the evolving career landscape confidently. These strategies not only equip individuals to meet current job demands but also prepare them for future shifts, ensuring they remain relevant and competitive.

Investing in continuous learning is akin to futureproofing one's career. It means staying updated with industry trends, acquiring new knowledge and skills, and, most importantly, maintaining a growth mindset. The willingness to learn, unlearn, and relearn has become a critical asset in the age of AI, and those who embrace this mindset will be better positioned to seize emerging opportunities for career advancement.

As we navigate this exciting and challenging AI-driven landscape, we must remember that while we must strive to adapt and learn continuously, we must also ensure that we don't lose sight of our distinct human qualities. Our adaptability, creativity, and innate ability to learn and grow are what makes us unique, and it is these qualities that will enable us to not only survive but thrive in the age of artificial intelligence.

[172] https://www.linkedin.com/pulse/adapting-changing-job-market-embracing-rise-ai-cara-cusack

[173] https://www.odysseytraining.com.au/tips-and-news/professional_development_tips/increase-your-employability-with-upskilling/

[174] https://www.zdnet.com/article/how-will-ai-impact-your-industry-pew-research-has-answers/

[175] https://www.forbes.com/sites/bernardmarr/2022/06/15/developing-the-most-in-demand-skills-for-the-future-of-work/?sh=143578e6b977

[176] https://www.linkedin.com/advice/0/how-do-you-leverage-online-learning-networking

[177] https://certiport.pearsonvue.com/About/The-value-of-certification.aspx

[178] https://www.australianenvironmentaleducation.com.au/about/hands-on-learning-in-classroom/#:~:text=Hands%20on%20Learning%20improves%20problem%20solving&text=Incorporating%20hands%2Don%20problem%2Dsolving,with%20problems%20in%20future%20programs.

[179] https://www.mindtools.com/a4wo118/smart-goals

[180] https://hbr.org/2019/02/making-learning-a-part-of-everyday-work

[181] https://lattice.com/library/how-and-when-to-revisit-your-goals

CHAPTER 7: ETHICS, MORALITY, AND AI

The Ethical Challenges Posed by AI in a Rapidly Evolving World

AI, with its transformative power, holds the potential to greatly improve our lives, streamline our work, and revolutionize our world. Yet, its growing influence necessitates a deep and serious consideration of the ethical dimensions that its deployment and development involve.

This chapter will venture into the often-nebulous realm of AI ethics, exploring the profound ethical issues and dilemmas that this technological revolution brings to the fore. These issues are manifold and complex, ranging from questions of privacy and data security to broader concerns about AI autonomy, the implications of machine learning, and the potential for algorithmic bias.

Addressing these ethical issues is not simply a matter of philosophical debate or theoretical importance—it has profound and practical implications for how we live, work, and interact in an AI-driven world. Therefore, we'll discuss why it is not just important, but indeed imperative, to confront these challenges head-on, to engage in these debates, and to ensure that ethics is embedded in the fabric of AI development and deployment.

In navigating this complex landscape, the objective is not to stifle innovation or decry technological progress, but rather to provide a compass for the path ahead. To this end, this chapter will outline strategies and propose frameworks for ethical AI, aiming to create a future where humans and AI can coexist harmoniously. In this envisioned future, AI systems will be designed and used in a way that respects human rights, upholds shared ethical principles, and serves the common good.

The challenges we face are significant, but so too are the opportunities. In the pages that follow, we'll seek to better understand these challenges and to propose ways to ensure that as we step into the future, we do so in a way that brings the best of our human values with us.

Addressing the ethical challenges posed by AI is essential for several reasons:

- Protecting human rights and values: Ensuring that AI technologies respect human rights and values is crucial for preserving our humanity and maintaining social cohesion in an AI-driven society. Whilst AI offers far-reaching benefits for humankind, it also has some serious risks that need addressing. These include further division between the privileged and unprivileged, erosion of individual freedoms via surveillance, and replacement of independent thought and judgement with automated control. Human rights are central to what it means to be human. Human rights frameworks and legislation were drafted and agreed upon with worldwide popular support in order to define liberties and entitlements that ensure every human being has the ability to live a life of dignity and liberty. Make no mistake that AI is redefining what it means to be human, and to date, human rights have so far been overlooked in the governance of AI around the world. [182]

- Building public trust: Addressing ethical concerns is vital for building public trust in AI technologies, fostering widespread adoption, and minimising resistance to change. We must engage in conversations and concentrate on increasing transparency as well as educating the public. To trust computer decisions, ethical or otherwise, people need to know how an AI system arrived at its conclusion and recommendations. Rachel Bellamy, IBM research manager for human-agent collaboration, says, "We will likely get to a point in the next five years when an AI system can better explain why it's telling you to do what it's recommending". AI developers must also be transparent about what the system is doing as it interacts with us. Is it gathering information about us from various places? Is it "looking" at our faces through a web camera to read our emotions? People need to have the ability to turn these functions off. Transparency through education is another effective way to build public trust. Misconceptions about what AI can and can't do are everywhere, and that erodes trust in the abilities it does possess. Also, a lack of clarity about which jobs AI might impact generates an additional level of distrust in the technology. For these reasons AI thought leaders and developers must move to educate the wider public and dispel any concern. [183]
- Ensuring equitable access and benefits: Addressing ethical challenges can help ensure that the benefits of AI are distributed fairly and equitably, minimising the risk of exacerbating existing social and economic inequalities. The lack of inclusive AI has proven harmful to businesses, both financially and reputationally, as well as to certain communities, in particular ethnic, cultural, ideological, and generational minorities. Many systems within society, including economic, social, or socioeconomic, have proven to be inequitable by design. Because inequality and inequity are often reflected in technologies, some AI can and has reinforced the marginalisation of certain groups, such as women, gender minorities, and racialized and low-income communities. AI-powered products and services may use biased data sets that reproduce this bias. AI should provide targeted assistance to those who need it most. For example, an organization that provides food aid could use an AI model to predict which areas will be hit hardest by a natural disaster before it happens. Education inequality is a primary concern for countries around the world. Students from disadvantaged backgrounds often have fewer resources available, making it difficult for them to keep up with their peers. AI is already helping in this space with personalised learning experiences, tracking attendance, and assistance with grading and marking. Health inequity is a significant issue in many parts of the world. AI has the potential to bridge this gap by making healthcare more accessible and affordable for

everyone. For example, AI algorithms can help healthcare providers diagnose diseases faster and more accurately than ever before, reducing wait times, reducing costs, and increasing access to care for all patients regardless of race or socio-economic status. [184]

- Promoting responsible innovation: Considering ethical implications in AI development, there needs to be encouragement, a framework, and government regulation and policy to set the parameters and guide responsible innovation that fosters a more sustainable and inclusive future for all. We are essentially witnessing an AI arms race by the big tech companies of the world to develop and deliver AI as quickly as possible to increase their revenue and service offerings. The general AI arms race is one thing, but the race we should all be paying attention to and demanding as individuals and companies is the race to build AI responsibly. Sundar Pichai, CEO of Google, wrote an opinion piece for the *Financial Times* on May 23, 2023, where he says the following:

> We are making sure we develop and deploy the technology responsibly, reflecting our deep commitment to earning the trust of our users. AI should be developed to benefit society while avoiding harmful applications. As AI evolves, so does our approach: this month we announced we'll provide ways to identify when we've used it to generate content in our services. AI needs to be regulated in a way that balances innovation and potential harms. With the technology now at an inflection point, I still believe AI is too important not to regulate and too important not to regulate well. Developing policy frameworks that anticipate potential harms and unlock benefits will require deep discussions between governments, industry experts, publishers, academia, and civil society. Continued investment in research and development for responsible AI will be important—as will ensuring AI is applied safely, especially where regulations are still evolving.

It's good to see companies such as Google making these claims, but we need to hold them to account where policy is lacking or not developed yet to in fact ensure they are innovating responsibly. [185]

Some of the most pressing ethical challenges associated with AI include the following:

- Privacy and surveillance: The widespread collection and use of personal data by AI systems raise concerns about privacy, surveillance, and the potential misuse of sensitive information. Privacy is the right to keep personal information confidential and free from unauthorised access. It is an essential human right and, today, more than ever, in the face of huge AI advances, important to address. The importance of privacy in the digital era cannot be overstated. It's necessary for personal autonomy, protection, and fairness. As AI becomes increasingly prevalent in our lives, we must remain vigilant in protecting our privacy to ensure that technology is used ethically and responsibly. AI systems require vast amounts of (personal) data, and if this data falls into the wrong hands, it can be used for nefarious purposes, such as identity theft or cyberbullying. AI-powered surveillance systems analyse massive volumes of data from a variety of sources, including cameras, social media, and other online sources. While the deployment of AI-based surveillance systems appears to be a significant weapon in the battle against crime and terrorism, it poses privacy and civil liberties concerns. Critics claim that these devices can be used to monitor and control individuals, potentially robbing them of their freedom and civil freedoms. Worse, the employment of AI-powered surveillance technologies is not always transparent. Individuals may be unaware when they are being observed or for what purpose. This lack of openness can weaken public faith in law enforcement and security services while also instilling fear in the general people. [186]

- Bias and discrimination: AI algorithms can perpetuate or exacerbate existing biases and discrimination if not properly designed and monitored, leading to unfair treatment of certain groups or individuals. AI systems are only as impartial as the data on which they are trained; if the data is biased, the final system will be as well. This can result in biased judgements based on criteria such as race, gender, or socioeconomic position. To avoid bias, AI systems must be educated on a wide range of data and constantly reviewed. The connection between bias and discrimination in AI and privacy may not be obvious at first look. After all, privacy is frequently regarded as a separate problem distinct from the protection of personal information and the right to be left alone. AI relies on data to make decisions and recommendations. This data is sourced from numerous platforms and sources, such as online activities, social media posts, and public documents, for example. We all know the internet can be a hazardous place with online sources generating fake content and points of view that are harmful to wider society. AI is trained on all of this. The good, the bad, and the flat-out factually incorrect. While this information may appear benign at first glance, it may disclose a great deal about a person's life, including ethnicity, gender, religion, and political convictions. As a result, if an AI system is prejudiced or discriminating, it might utilise this data to reinforce its prejudices, resulting in unfair or even harmful outcomes for individuals. [187]

- Transparency and accountability: The complexity and opacity of certain AI systems, particularly deep learning models, can make it challenging to understand how decisions are made, raising questions about transparency and accountability. One of the main reasons people fear AI is that it can be hard to explain. AI data-driven technologies such as machine learning and the relationship between input and output can cause our imaginations to wander, as they are hard to explain. The point of transparent AI is to enable the output of an AI model to be explainable and communicated clearly in plain language to the general public. Transparent AI can be thought of as explainable AI. It should allow humans to see if the models have been thoroughly tested and make sense, and that they can understand why the AI came to deliver the output they receive. Now this doesn't mean developers should start posting AI algorithms or code snippets online. This is being discussed in some parts of the world to address transparency. However, the majority of people who interact with AI do not understand raw lines of computer programming code. The algorithmic code would make no sense to them. The level of transparency should also be delivered in relation to how much of an impact AI has on our lives. If I was using a GPT model to write a response to a nasty email I received, that model would not need as much scrutiny as say an AI model that is used to grant me a bank loan or recommend a medical treatment during a visit to my doctor. [188]

- Autonomy and agency: As AI systems increasingly make decisions on our behalf, concerns arise about the potential erosion of human autonomy and agency, as well as the ethical implications of delegating critical decisions to machines. As we cede decision-making on key aspects in life to code-driven tools, those of us who function in this digital world sacrifice, to varying degrees, our independence, right to privacy, and power over choice. I know for a fact that as I write this it's a Friday afternoon, and I will in fact get a notification shortly from a well-known food delivery service asking me what new cuisine in my local area I would like to try tonight. It's worked out that Fridays are when I least feel like cooking and when I order take out the most. Many of us use AI in this manner to stay competitive, participate socially and professionally in the world, be entertained, and get things done. We hand over some control of our lives because of the perceived advantages we gain via digital tool: efficiency, convenience, superior pattern recognition, data storage, and search-and-find capabilities. Loss of human agency and autonomy could be the worst outcome for humanity in the age of AI as we trade context and control over our lives and decisions to instant, low-friction, convenient technologies. Our blind dependence on digital technologies is deepening as automated systems get more complex and permeate our lives silently and with greater ease due to the perceived convenience. [189]

- Job displacement and the future of work: AI's potential to automate numerous jobs raises ethical concerns about the impact on employment, social stability, and economic inequality. In May 2023 IBM put a pause on hiring nearly 7,800 jobs that could be replaced by AI. In early June, barely two weeks later, BT announced it would cut up to 55,000 jobs by 2030 with about 10,000 to be replaced by AI. These announcements aren't entirely surprising. If businesses are to not only survive but thrive in the face of rapid technological advancement, they must adapt to these technological shifts in order to remain competitive and profitable. Doom-and-gloom predictions about job losses are never far from mainstream media. Take, for example, typing. The typing profession grew in popularity with the introduction of computers and then fell away and nearly went extinct. Due to the same trends and same technology, we saw demand rise for web designers, graphic designers, and copyeditors. Computers birthed countless sectors and transformed our way of life. AI could do this again if we strategically guide it. We need to understand what jobs are at risk and how AI will deliver those jobs. Repetitive data input and administrative operations are obvious targets for AI, likewise for manufacturing and logistics. AI and automation are most useful alongside human-based roles instead of complete replacement. Humans can offer the complex decision-making skills that machines lack. Some jobs, however, will be lost. This is why governments, educational institutions, and companies need to come together and develop comprehensive retraining and upskilling programmes and job placement support to assist displaced people's transition to more future-proof roles. [190]

To address the ethical challenges posed by AI, consider the following strategies:

- Develop and implement ethical guidelines and frameworks: Establish clear ethical guidelines and frameworks for AI development and use, taking into account diverse perspectives and values. Encourage AI developers and users to adhere to these guidelines and promote ethical AI practices. None of the previous technologies that humanity has created can compare to artificial intelligence. It will spread faster than the internet and have a bigger impact on society and the economy than fossil fuels, and, eventually, it's likely to slip from human control and decide its own future. This is why we must design AI with purpose and develop it ethically and responsibly. Ethics centres around the notion that we must take responsibility for our actions and their impact on the world and that we should act in ways that are beneficial and not harmful. AI should give us more freedom and not take less or create the feeling of less. This is why it must be designed ethically and responsibly so that we can understand when we are interacting with it, how it works, and how it will affect us, so we can make informed decisions about whether to use it and how to use it. AI developers must tackle the ethical issues that arise from the mass collection, analysis, and use of data, especially when data is used to train the machine learning models behind AI platforms. [191]

- Promote transparency and accountability: Encourage transparency in AI algorithms and decision-making processes, enabling individuals to understand and scrutinize how decisions are made. Establish clear lines of accountability for the outcomes and impacts of AI systems. As AI and algorithms become further embedded into our lives, there needs to be more transparency about when AI is used and what it is used for. Transparency is a cornerstone of earning the trust of consumers, clients, and the general public. Transparency, though, is not just about informing people when they are interacting with AI, but also communicating with people about why an AI-based solution was chosen, how it was developed and designed, how the framework around its monitoring and updating was deployed, and the conditions under which it may be retired. Transparency is not one exercise; it is or should be treated as a chain that travels from the designers and developers through to the people it impacts. [192]

- Prioritise fairness and inclusivity: Actively work to minimize bias and discrimination in AI systems by prioritising fairness and inclusivity in algorithm design, data collection, and system deployment. Regularly audit AI systems to identify and mitigate potential biases. AI systems are built on huge lakes of data, and they continually learn from that data. If that data is skewed due to the collection parameters or even from the point of view of the person building the AI using the data, it can have unforeseen consequences for the rest of us that use that AI. Diversity, fairness, and inclusivity is of great importance because we want to ensure that when AI makes a decision, it can make it accurately and fairly. Recent studies have shown that only 15 percent of AI researchers at Meta and just 10 percent at Google are women. Less than 5 percent of workers at both these companies are Black, so it's not hard to see, then, that the AI products these companies produce could in fact have unplanned biases built in. In light of the fact that there may not be enough women or people of colour working in these technology-based roles, we must then ensure that adequate testing and auditing of AI systems take place to identify, address, and rectify any biases that could be present in these algorithms and platforms before they are released to the general public with potentially disastrous outcomes. [193]

- Foster interdisciplinary collaboration: Encourage collaboration between AI developers, ethicists, policymakers, and other stakeholders to ensure that diverse perspectives and expertise are integrated into the development and deployment of AI technologies. Interdisciplinary research and development have the potential to overcome disciplinary boundaries and narrow views to promote new approaches that are more inclusive and integrated and that better reflect the complex reality of AI in society today. For example, we can't expect a government policymaker to understand the nuances of machine learning and neural networks, just as we can't expect an AI engineer to understand the delicate societal balance of fairness, diversity, and inclusion strategies. By working in groups where the greatest minds of a wide range of sectors and specialities come together to share their knowledge, we can get input into overarching strategies for the development and outcomes of this amazing new technology to protect society from harmful AI interactions. [194]

- Invest in education and public awareness: Promote education and public awareness of the ethical challenges posed by AI, fostering a more informed and engaged society that can collectively navigate the complex ethical landscape of AI. Earlier in the book I wrote about social media and its negative effects on people. Only now are we understanding the harm social media can have on young people's development both mentally and physically. We must avoid making similar mistakes with AI development. I believe governments, private companies, and research and education institutions must step in and step up to educate the general public and raise awareness around AI both as a topic and regarding how embedded AI already is in our lives. We don't know the harms and unintended consequences this technology may deliver years from now, which is why education is so important. Regulation is only half the job. A more aware and tech-literate public is not a bad thing and will help people make more informed decisions about their use of AI as well as their children. [195]

In conclusion, the ethical challenges borne out of the increasing pervasiveness of AI demand our collective attention and engagement. Preserving our humanity in this new era is contingent on our ability to address these challenges head-on, carving out a landscape where AI and humans can coexist harmoniously, enriching and augmenting each other rather than supplanting one another.

Establishing robust ethical guidelines is a crucial step in this direction. These guidelines act as our moral compass, setting the parameters within which AI should operate to ensure it aligns with our shared values and principles. They guide AI design and deployment, preventing harm and fostering a trust-based relationship between humans and AI technologies.

Alongside ethical guidelines, promoting transparency and accountability is fundamental. AI should not be a black box whose workings are mysterious and incomprehensible. Ensuring transparency allows us to understand and validate AI's decisions, while accountability puts the onus on the creators and users of AI to answer for its outcomes. Together, these principles ensure that AI serves its intended purpose, aiding humanity rather than undermining it.

Moreover, our ethical considerations must encompass a strong focus on fairness and inclusivity. AI has the potential to either bridge or widen social disparities, depending on how we navigate its deployment. It's paramount that we use AI to level the playing field, offering equitable access to its benefits and mitigating its potential drawbacks. This requires consciously working to eliminate biases in AI systems and ensuring they are representative of and beneficial to all sectors of society.

The ethical journey through the AI landscape is complex and multi-faceted, demanding a convergence of perspectives from individuals, communities, organisations, and governments. In the following chapters, we will further explore the strategies essential for maintaining our humanity in the face of the digital age. We'll delve into the pivotal role of collaboration, education, and public policy in shaping a future where the scales are balanced: acknowledging the immense benefits of AI and addressing its risks, all the while preserving and celebrating our unique human qualities and values.

This journey of ethical coexistence with AI is not a destination but a continual process. As we tread this path, it is our shared responsibility to ensure that as we leverage the powers of artificial intelligence, we remain mindful of our humanity, champion our shared values, and envisage a future where technology is truly in service of humanity.

[182] https://ts2.space/en/ai-and-human-rights-ensuring-that-intelligent-machines-respect-fundamental-values/

[183] https://www.ibm.com/watson/advantage-reports/future-of-artificial-intelligence/building-trust-in-ai.html

[184] https://www.gendereconomy.org/wp-content/uploads/2021/09/An-Equity-Lens-on-Artificial-Intelligence-Public-Version-English-1.pdf

[185] https://www.ft.com/content/8be1a975-e5e0-417d-af51-78af17ef4b79

[186] https://www.thedigitalspeaker.com/privacy-age-ai-risks-challenges-solutions/#:~:text=The%20Use%20of%20AI%20in,to%20privacy%20and%20civil%20liberties.

[187] https://www.thedigitalspeaker.com/privacy-age-ai-risks-challenges-solutions/#:~:text=The%20Use%20of%20AI%20in,to%20privacy%20and%20civil%20liberties.

[188]https://www2.deloitte.com/content/dam/Deloitte/nl/Documents/innovatie/deloitte-nl-innovation-bringing-transparency-and-ethics-into-ai.pdf

[189] https://www.pewresearch.org/internet/2018/12/10/concerns-about-human-agency-evolution-and-survival/

[190] https://www.theguardian.com/commentisfree/2023/may/22/ai-jobs-policies

[191] https://ethics.org.au/a-framework-for-ethical-ai/#:~:text=Purpose%20must%20be%20central%20to,is%20worthwhile%20and%20achieved%20ethically.

[192] https://hbr.org/2022/06/building-transparency-into-ai-projects

[193] https://www.forbes.com/sites/forbestechcouncil/2021/03/16/diversity-and-inclusion-in-ai/?sh=6d1146215823

[194] https://www.linkedin.com/pulse/ai-interdisciplinary-rd-robb-bush/

[195] https://diginomica.com/ai-regulation-priority-so-awareness-and-education-lets-not-repeat-same-mistakes

Human Values and Moral Considerations in AI Development

In a rapidly evolving digital landscape, the integration of artificial intelligence into everyday life is no longer a distant possibility but a tangible reality. From personalised healthcare treatments to intelligent transportation systems, AI's influence is pervasive and growing. However, with this technological progression comes a responsibility to ensure that AI does not just serve the interests of efficiency and automation but also adheres to the very human values and moral considerations that define our society.

The relationship between AI and human ethics is intricate and multifaceted. On one hand, AI has the potential to elevate human life, providing innovative solutions to age-old problems, enhancing convenience, and even saving lives. On the other hand, without careful consideration of ethical principles, AI can unintentionally perpetuate biases, infringe on privacy, and create disparities that exacerbate social inequalities.

The development of AI is not merely a technical challenge but a profoundly moral one. Engineers, policymakers, ethicists, and society at large must work in concert to navigate the fine balance between technological advancement and ethical integrity. This endeavour involves establishing clear ethical guidelines that reflect core human values such as fairness, transparency, privacy, and accountability. It demands interdisciplinary collaboration, where technological expertise meets ethical philosophy to create AI systems that resonate with our shared human ideals.

Furthermore, the dynamic nature of technology necessitates ongoing vigilance and adaptability. Ethical considerations must be fluid and responsive to the evolving landscape of AI, adapting to new developments and addressing unforeseen challenges. Governments, industry leaders, and communities must be engaged in an ongoing dialogue, setting regulations, educating the public, and ensuring that ethical AI is not just an aspiration but a lived reality.

This chapter will delve deeper into these critical aspects, examining the inherent tensions and synergies between AI and human values. Through an exploration of real-world examples, theoretical frameworks, and practical strategies, we will shed light on how to embed human values and morals into AI systems. In doing so, we will take meaningful steps toward a future where AI not only transforms our capabilities but enriches our lives, ensuring a more humane, inclusive, and responsible coexistence with technology.

Incorporating human values and morals in AI development is essential for several reasons:

- Maintaining social cohesion: Ensuring that AI technologies respect and uphold human values and morals helps maintain social cohesion and promote a shared understanding of what is right and wrong in an AI-driven society. Digitalisation and AI have become amplifiers for existing social inequalities. China, for example, has a very different relationship with technology than the rest of the world. They use digitalisation to control their people via a social scoring system. They track people using one of the largest surveillance systems in the world. If you jaywalk, the fine is withdrawn from your bank account before you even arrive at your destination. Have you stayed out at the pub drinking with your friends a few nights this week and maybe called in sick to work as a result? This will see your social score drop, and in some instances the scores of the friends you were out with will drop as well. China has access to so much data, which is the foundation for a system like this. To avoid this type of Orwellian future in Western society, we need to include everyone in the broader development of AI. We can do this through participatory design, increasing data literacy, and improving digital education from elementary school onwards. We must build AI systems that create more inclusive and equitable societies. AI systems can recognise and reward individuals for their contributions to society regardless of their background or income level and can provide access to services and resources to those who need it most. AI can actually recognise the root cause of inequality and highlight it so we can work with AI to develop better, more meaningful outcomes and actually address these issues, now that we have access to the computing power that could in fact help to solve them. [196]

- Building public trust: Addressing ethical concerns and aligning AI systems with human values is vital for building public trust and acceptance of AI technologies. It is government's role to raise public awareness of what AI is, what it isn't, and what it can be used for. This is key to developing public acceptance and understanding of the technology. I was very pleased to see that my very own local NSW state government has already developed an AI policy and included the below around building public trust in AI:

> It is Government's responsibility to use smart technologies to deliver better services and to identify and respond to community concerns, including those relating to privacy, security, and ethical considerations.
>
> There are already many applications of AI in government that benefit citizens, including for traffic management, chatbots in customer service centres and better-designed health services. The private sector routinely uses data for targeted service delivery and marketing purposes. Often, the public may not be aware that their data is being used for AI solutions that have direct and demonstrable benefits.
>
> To this effect, the NSW Government will establish a new AI Review Committee that will review project plans and assist with implementation to ensure solutions meet the government's high ethical standards.
>
> This Strategy recognises that more needs to be done to provide assurance to the community that Government will always strive to ensure the safe use of AI,

finding the balance between opportunity and risk, and protecting customers and citizen's privacy and security. [197]

- Ensuring equitable access and benefits: By embedding human values and morals in AI development, we can help ensure that the benefits of AI technologies are fairly distributed, minimising the risk of exacerbating existing social and economic inequalities. It is important to investigate and interrogate the assumptions about collected data and AI processes. At every step of the process, we must look at where a human may be biased to ensure we design that out. That investigation and interrogation includes critically analysing the data sets used to inform AI systems. Understanding the data sources and how the data is formed up is crucial in order to respond to inquiries like, "How is the data made up?" "Does it include a broad range of stakeholders?" "What is the most effective approach for using that data in a model to reduce bias and increase fairness?" Equitable AI aims to produce fairer outcomes, increase opportunities, and improve workplace success for all workers, regardless of race, ethnicity, disability, age, gender identity or expression, religion, sexual orientation, or economic status. [198]
- Promoting responsible innovation: Considering ethical implications and human values in AI development can encourage responsible innovation, fostering a more sustainable and inclusive future for all. Innovation typically arises due to uncertainty and change. Innovation requires responsible thinking and development through flexibility, creativity, and leadership. AI developers must start to consider as early in the development phase as possible who needs to be involved in the design process. This is where we return to diversity and inclusion. We need a diverse range of perspectives in order to deliver fair, equitable, and responsible solutions. Responsible AI means designing, developing, and deploying AI with good intentions to empower employees and businesses and fairly impact customers and society—allowing companies to engender trust and scale AI with confidence. [199]

To ensure that human values and morals are embedded in AI development, consider the following strategies:

- Establish ethical guidelines and frameworks: Develop and implement ethical guidelines and frameworks for AI development that prioritise human values and morals. Encourage AI developers, practitioners, and users to adhere to these guidelines and promote ethical AI practices. AI, unlike other technologies, is not the kind of technology we can afford to release into the world and then wait and see what happens before regulating it. We need guidelines and frameworks for developers and users so that AI is both designed and used with purpose, in an ethical manner and responsibly. [200]
- Foster interdisciplinary collaboration: Encourage collaboration between AI developers, ethicists, philosophers, policymakers, and other stakeholders

to ensure that diverse perspectives and expertise inform the development and deployment of AI technologies. The development of AI is not a task for any single discipline, industry, or field. It requires the combined efforts of experts in linguistics, cognitive science, policy and governance, computer programming, and more. Each field brings unique insights and specialist knowledge to the table to contribute to a more comprehensive and well-thought-out delivery of AI to the world. Interdisciplinary collaboration is not without its challenges though: communication barriers, the fact that such deep specialists can have trouble seeing issues from another point of view, terminology and methodology challenges, and simply coordinating efforts between teams in the face of a very complex project. To overcome these challenges, it's important to make all team members and each agency feel heard, create a common language that all parties can understand, and have mutual respect for everyone who is, at the simplest level, aiming for the same shared outcome. [201]

- Welcome public and stakeholder input: Seek input from the public and diverse stakeholders in the development and deployment of AI technologies, ensuring that AI systems align with the values and expectations of the communities they serve. Stakeholders are anyone who can affect or be affected by your AI project, such as employees, partners, suppliers, regulators, investors, or society at large. We need to identify who they are, what their interests and concerns are, and how they can influence or be influenced by your AI project. We also need to consider the impact of AI on different groups of people, such as those who are vulnerable or marginalised, and ensure they are heard and respected. All these people and groups should be involved or canvassed during the design and development of your AI platform, as their input and participation are crucial at every stage. We need to consult them on the objectives, methods, criteria, and indicators of our AI projects and ensure that they reflect human rights principles and values. [202]

Several organisations and initiatives are actively working to incorporate human values and morals into AI development. Some notable examples include the following:

- The Partnership on AI: A multi-stakeholder organization that brings together AI developers, researchers, ethicists, policymakers, and other stakeholders to develop best practices and ethical guidelines for AI technologies. Their website states the following:

    Partnership on AI (PAI) is a non-profit partnership of academic, civil society, industry, and media organisations creating solutions so that AI advances positive outcomes for people and society. By convening diverse, international stakeholders, we seek to pool collective wisdom to make change. We are not a trade group or advocacy organization.

    We develop tools, recommendations, and other resources by inviting voices from across the AI community and beyond to share insights that can be synthesized into actionable guidance. We then work to drive adoption in practice, inform public policy, and advance public understanding. Through dialogue, research, and education, PAI is addressing the most important and difficult questions concerning the future of AI.

Our Mission
Bringing diverse voices together across global sectors, disciplines, and demographics so developments in AI advance positive outcomes for people and society.

Our Vision
A future where Artificial Intelligence empowers humanity by contributing to a more just, equitable, and prosperous world. [203]

- AI Ethics Guidelines by the European Commission: A set of guidelines developed by the European Commission that outline key ethical principles, such as transparency, accountability, and human oversight, for AI development and use. Their website lists seven key requirements that AI systems should meet in order to be deemed trustworthy. This list includes the following:

    1. Human agency and oversight: AI systems should empower human beings, allowing them to make informed decisions and fostering their fundamental rights. At the same time, proper oversight mechanisms need to be ensured, which can be achieved through human-in-the-loop, human-on-the-loop, and human-in-command approaches.
    2. Technical robustness and safety: AI systems need to be resilient and secure. They need to be safe, ensuring a fall-back plan in case something goes wrong, as well as being accurate, reliable and reproducible. That is the only way to ensure that unintentional harm can be minimized and prevented.
    3. Privacy and data governance: besides ensuring full respect for privacy and data protection, adequate data governance mechanisms must also be ensured, taking into account the quality and integrity of the data and ensuring legitimised access to data.
    4. Transparency: the data, system, and AI business models should be transparent. Traceability mechanisms can help achieve this. Moreover, AI systems and their decisions should be explained in a manner adapted to the stakeholder concerned. Humans need to be aware that they are interacting with an AI system and must be informed of the system's capabilities and limitations.
    5. Diversity, non-discrimination, and fairness: Unfair bias must be avoided, as it could have multiple negative implications, from the marginalization of vulnerable groups, to the exacerbation of prejudice and discrimination. Fostering diversity, AI systems should be accessible to all, regardless of any disability, and involve relevant stakeholders throughout their entire life circle.
    6. Societal and environmental well-being: AI systems should benefit all human beings, including future generations. It must hence be ensured that they are sustainable and environmentally friendly. Moreover, they

should take into account the environment, including other living beings, and their social and societal impact should be carefully considered.

7. Accountability: Mechanisms should be put in place to ensure responsibility and accountability for AI systems and their outcomes. Auditability, which enables the assessment of algorithms, data, and design processes, plays a key role therein, especially in critical applications. Moreover, adequate and accessible redress should be ensured. [204]

- OpenAI's Charter: A guiding document that outlines OpenAI's commitment to ensuring that AI technologies are developed and deployed in ways that benefit all of humanity, prioritising long-term safety and technical leadership. Their website reads as follows:

This document reflects the strategy we've refined over the past two years, including feedback from many people internal and external to OpenAI. The timeline to AGI remains uncertain, but our Charter will guide us in acting in the best interests of humanity throughout its development.

OpenAI's mission is to ensure that artificial general intelligence (AGI)—by which we mean highly autonomous systems that outperform humans at most economically valuable work—benefits all of humanity. We will attempt to directly build safe and beneficial AGI, but will also consider our mission fulfilled if our work aids others to achieve this outcome. To that end, we commit to the following principles:

Broadly distributed benefits
We commit to use any influence we obtain over AGI's deployment to ensure it is used for the benefit of all, and to avoid enabling uses of AI or AGI that harm humanity or unduly concentrate power.

Our primary fiduciary duty is to humanity. We anticipate needing to marshal substantial resources to fulfill our mission, but will always diligently act to minimize conflicts of interest among our employees and stakeholders that could compromise broad benefit.

Long-term safety
We are committed to doing the research required to make AGI safe, and to driving the broad adoption of such research across the AI community.

We are concerned about late-stage AGI development becoming a competitive race without time for adequate safety precautions. Therefore, if a value-aligned, safety-conscious project comes close to building AGI before we do, we commit to stop competing with and start assisting this project. We will work out specifics in case-by-case agreements, but a typical triggering condition might be "a better-than-even chance of success in the next two years."

Technical leadership
To be effective at addressing AGI's impact on society, OpenAI must be on the cutting edge of AI capabilities—policy and safety advocacy alone would be insufficient.

We believe that AI will have broad societal impact before AGI, and we'll strive to lead in those areas that are directly aligned with our mission and expertise.

Cooperative orientation
We will actively cooperate with other research and policy institutions; we seek to create a global community working together to address AGI's global challenges.

We are committed to providing public goods that help society navigate the path to AGI. Today this includes publishing most of our AI research, but we expect that safety and security concerns will reduce our traditional publishing in the future, while increasing the importance of sharing safety, policy, and standards research. [205]

In conclusion, the integration of human values and morals into the very fabric of AI development is not only beneficial but vital for creating a future where AI technologies align with our ethical principles and contribute to a more humane, inclusive, and responsible society. This necessity is amplified by the pervasiveness of AI in various aspects of our lives, influencing our decision-making processes, interpersonal relationships, and professional environments and even our perception of the world.

Establishing ethical guidelines is one of the foremost steps towards this objective. These guidelines provide a structured approach towards determining what behaviours and outcomes are acceptable from AI systems. They ensure that human rights, dignity, and ethical considerations remain paramount as we develop and deploy these advanced technologies. Guidelines must be living documents, evolving in step with technological advancements and societal changes, thus maintaining their relevance and effectiveness over time.

Fostering interdisciplinary collaboration is another crucial aspect of this endeavour. The development and implementation of AI is not just a technical challenge; it is a socio-technical challenge that requires diverse perspectives. By encouraging collaboration between ethicists, psychologists, sociologists, technologists, and other stakeholders, we can address the ethical implications of AI from a more holistic viewpoint. Such collaboration enables us to create technologies that respect and uphold human values, rather than undermining them.

Furthermore, prioritising fairness, transparency, and accountability in AI systems ensures that these technologies are used responsibly. Fairness ensures that AI does not perpetuate biases or inequalities but instead actively works towards reducing them. Transparency involves the right to understand how AI systems make decisions, particularly those that significantly impact human lives. Accountability, on the other hand, emphasizes that developers and users of AI should be answerable for the consequences of their actions, fostering a culture of responsibility.

By ensuring that AI technologies uphold and reflect our values and morals, we set the stage for a harmonious coexistence between humans and AI. Such a future not only leverages the transformative potential of AI but also safeguards our human essence, enabling us to use technology as a tool for enhancement, rather than a threat to our humanity. As we continue to explore the intricate landscape of artificial intelligence, let us remain steadfast in prioritising ethical considerations, upholding human dignity, and fostering a society where technology serves humanity.

[196] https://www.belfercenter.org/publication/impact-ai-and-digitalization-social-cohesion

[197] https://www.digital.nsw.gov.au/policy/artificial-intelligence/artificial-intelligence-strategy/building-public-trust

[198] https://www.technologyreview.com/2021/05/18/1024910/evolving-to-a-more-equitable-ai/

[199] https://www.ucl.ac.uk/responsible-innovation/what-responsible-innovation

[200] https://ethics.org.au/a-framework-for-ethical-ai/

[201] https://www.linkedin.com/pulse/proving-we-care-interdisciplinary-collaboration-key-creating-galvin/

[202] https://www.linkedin.com/advice/0/what-best-practices-engaging-stakeholders-1e#:~:text=You%20need%20to%20involve%20your,human%20rights%20principles%20and%20values.

[203] https://partnershiponai.org/

[204] https://digital-strategy.ec.europa.eu/en/library/ethics-guidelines-trustworthy-ai

[205] https://openai.com/charter

The Role of Governments, Organisations, and Individuals in Ethical AI

As artificial intelligence continues to weave its way into the fabric of daily life, the ethical implications of AI become not only a concern of computer scientists and engineers but a shared responsibility for governments, organisations, and individuals alike. Ensuring that AI technologies align with our moral principles requires a concerted effort and collaboration across various domains of society. This chapter will embark on an exploration of the shared responsibilities and proactive measures that different stakeholders can take to contribute to a more ethical, inclusive, and responsible future with AI.

Governments play a vital role in laying down the legal and regulatory framework within which AI operates. They are tasked with establishing clear guidelines and enforcement mechanisms that prevent misuse, discrimination, and harmful consequences of AI applications. The balance between fostering innovation and protecting societal values often requires nuanced understanding, intergovernmental collaboration, and public consultation.

Organisations, whether they are private corporations or nonprofit entities, are at the frontline of AI implementation. Their choices in design, development, and deployment of AI systems have direct consequences on the lives of consumers and society at large. Hence, they must embed ethical considerations into their business strategies, development processes, and operational protocols. This involves considering the long-term social implications of their technologies, ensuring transparency, fairness, and privacy, and actively engaging with various stakeholders, including employees, customers, regulators, and the community.

Individuals, as users and beneficiaries of AI, also hold significant influence. The choices we make as consumers, professionals, and citizens shape the way AI technologies are developed and utilised. Active participation, education, and awareness can empower individuals to make informed decisions, engage in meaningful dialogue with tech providers, and advocate for ethical practices. Individuals' voices and choices send signals to both organisations and governments, reinforcing ethical norms and societal values.

Furthermore, academia and research institutions are essential contributors in shaping the ethical landscape of AI. Through interdisciplinary research, open dialogues, and education, they facilitate the creation of ethical principles, explore the societal implications of AI, and nurture the next generation of responsible AI practitioners.

The path to ethical AI is complex and multifaceted, involving various stakeholders operating within a dynamic and interdependent ecosystem. It requires a continual commitment to learning, dialogue, adaptation, and collaboration. In this chapter we will delve deeper into the strategies and challenges that illustrate how governments, organisations, individuals, and other stakeholders can work together to build an AI-driven world that not only harnesses the technological potential but also upholds and advances our shared human values.

Governments play a critical role in shaping the development and use of AI technologies within their jurisdictions. To promote ethical AI, governments can do the following:

- Develop and implement policy frameworks and regulations: Establish policy frameworks and regulations that prioritise ethical principles, such as transparency, accountability, and fairness, in AI development and use. Effective regulation and policy frameworks are necessary to ensure that potential risks are managed whilst still being flexible enough to enable innovation to flourish and opportunities to be realised. At the time of writing this book (2023), there is no specific legislation in force anywhere in the world we are aware of that is designed to regulate AI development. We are likely to see two forms of legislation developed over time. One is the general regulations which will govern AI, dependant on its application. The second is sector-specific regulations, which would govern AI when it is used in a particular sector. Speaking as a citizen of Australia, whatever regulation our government puts in place will need to be in harmony with those of other governments from around the world to avoid unnecessary red tape and disruption to our local tech sector and its ability to take advantage of AI-enabled systems and the economies of scale and global growth of AI solutions. [206]
- Invest in AI research and development: Support research and development in AI ethics, safety, and explainability to advance the understanding and implementation of ethical AI technologies. Governments from around the world are racing to invest in AI. In 2023 the Australian government committed $41.2 million to support the responsible deployment of AI in the national economy. [207] The UK government has also announced a series of investments totalling £54 million to support the UK's AI and data science workforce and develop trustworthy and secure AI. [208] The US has announced $140 million to create seven artificial intelligence research hubs and released new guidance on AI. The aim is to curtail risks associated with AI as the technology rapidly develops and to remind AI companies that they can help to reduce harm early on in this journey. [209]
- Foster public engagement and dialogue: Encourage public engagement and dialogue around AI ethics, providing opportunities for citizens to contribute to the development of ethical AI policies and regulations. The inherent opacity and rapid diffusion of AI and machine learning have prompted much debate about how these technologies should be governed and which actors and values should be involved in shaping governance. Responsible engagement by AI developers and governments requires public engagement and a prior debate with society due to the fact that these technologies permeate all layers of the social fabric and can impact greater social cohesion. Proactive approaches to

this challenge must emphasize dialogue across stakeholder groups and the inclusion of diverse perspectives in the design and monitoring of AI implementations. Public dialogues and consultations will help establish a democratic mandate to govern AI. To guarantee that the interests of the general public are taken into account, the government and those establishing AI committees should appoint "public champions", those who excel in bridging the gap between the general population and the scientific and technological elite. [210]

- Promote digital literacy and AI education: Support digital literacy and AI education initiatives to ensure that citizens are equipped to understand and navigate the ethical challenges posed by AI technologies. The digital age has brought with it a whole new language. The younger generations who have largely grown up as digital natives, having only known a life with digital technologies, are very literate in using and understanding these platforms. However, the older generations can feel excluded, as they lack the technical skills and confidence to use them or even access them. Governments should use data to ensure it addresses digital inclusion and that everyone knows how to use these new technologies and has a base-level understanding of how these technologies work and when they are in fact engaging with technology such as AI. The government can use data for inclusion in three ways: (1) to understand how their citizens are interacting with technology, (2) to identify vulnerable groups of people and communities, and (3) to better understand the needs of its citizens. [211]

Organisations, including businesses, research institutions, and non-governmental organisations, are responsible for developing and deploying AI technologies. To promote ethical AI, organisations can do the following:

- Adopt ethical guidelines and frameworks: Implement ethical guidelines and frameworks that prioritise human values and morals in AI development and use. From speech recognition and chatbots to robotic automation and natural language processing, the application of AI technologies by private businesses is proliferating daily. However, corporate ethics statements say very little about the implications of AI use within their own business or for the consumers they serve. Businesses utilizing this technology must have checks and balances in place, allow for the challenge of AI decisions when necessary, and ensure that the right governance is in place. Physical danger (for instance, autonomous vehicles), plagiarism (AI-powered art and music), fraud (online banking), and privacy law violations (e-commerce systems) are a few examples of common ethical dilemmas associated with AI. Building trust and ensuring that everyone is aware of the potential impact of AI on the organization can be achieved by having open and honest conversations with employees and stakeholders about the use of AI in the workplace. The ethical implications on corporate AI use are a moving target; it's too late to put the AI genie back in the bottle, and a wait-and-see approach simply won't work. Businesses must document and enforce clear ethical guardrails now and understand tweaks to their policies and frameworks will be needed regularly and for some time as this technology continues to evolve. [212]

- Foster interdisciplinary collaboration: Encourage collaboration between AI developers, ethicists, and other stakeholders to ensure that diverse perspectives and expertise inform the development and deployment of AI technologies. Even businesses looking to competitors or adjacent industries would likely learn a lot, as we are all on a similar journey to understand how to best utilise this technology in a safe and efficient manner. Instead of trying to solve issues internally and everyone going through this journey separately, it's beneficial to look sideways and see what others are doing around your company or industry to either develop or deploy AI in a safe way.

- Invest in AI ethics training and education: Provide AI ethics training and education to employees, ensuring that they are aware of the ethical implications of AI technologies and are equipped to make responsible decisions. More issues, both big and small, can be resolved throughout the organization if more people are knowledgeable about AI and can start to participate and contribute to the process. The goal should be to democratise this skill set and give everyone the basic understanding to engage with AI. Having staff upskilled in AI and even specialists such as data scientists and machine learning power users embedded throughout your business will become a competitive advantage. There should also be training on how AI can go off the map and go wrong, including education on bad and biased data and their effect on AI systems. Educating employees provides them more opportunities to stay up-to-date as the economy starts to require more and more AI-educated roles. Education on AI is also a huge part of reskilling people as the potential for job losses and an evolving job market is a talking point around the world, which we discuss in depth in the following chapter. [213]

- Monitor and audit AI systems: Regularly monitor and audit AI systems to identify and mitigate potential ethical risks, including biases, discrimination, and privacy violations. Monitoring the application of AI tools and ensuring that ethical guidelines are rigorously enforced and concerns addressed when the occasion arises is essential, and there are two factors to consider when auditing an AI system. The first is compliance: risk assessment related to an AI system's compliance with legal, regulatory, ethical, and social considerations. The second is technology: risk assessment related to technical capabilities, including machine learning, security standards, and model performance. [214]

Individuals play an essential role in shaping the ethical landscape of AI technologies through their actions, choices, and influence. To promote ethical AI, individuals can do the following:

- Stay informed and educated: Develop an understanding of AI technologies and their ethical implications, engaging in ongoing learning and dialogue around AI ethics. One of the easiest ways to keep up with AI developments is to follow online resources that provide news, insights, tutorials, and courses on a range of AI topics. Even attending events and webinars that showcase the latest research and application of AI is beneficial. You can network and talk to people deep in the space to develop your understanding. Lastly, consider enrolling in online courses that teach you the fundamentals of AI topics, such as machine learning, deep learning, or natural language processing. [215]

- Advocate for ethical AI: Advocate for ethical AI practices within their communities, workplaces, and networks, promoting awareness and encouraging responsible AI development and use. Promote the practice of good data management to mitigate potential bias and ask your general management, data, and AI teams to incorporate privacy by design principles into the design and build phases of AI products. Create ethics governance structures and ensure accountability is installed for AI systems. Ask employers or developers, "Who is responsible and to be held accountable for ethical issues in AI?" Build internal or external committees responsible for ethical AI deployment. [216]

- Participate in public discussions and decision-making: Take part in public discussions and decision-making processes related to AI ethics, sharing perspectives, and contributing to the development of ethical AI policies and regulations. Participating in public discussions provides an avenue to share your insights, concerns, and suggestions about the ethical implications of AI technologies. By contributing your unique viewpoint, you help broaden the understanding of AI's potential benefits and risks, ensuring that decisions are well-informed and considerate of a wide range of perspectives. Engagement in these discussions fosters transparency, accountability, and responsible AI development. When stakeholders from different backgrounds and fields come together to deliberate on AI ethics, it helps create a holistic understanding of the complex challenges and opportunities AI presents. This collective knowledge is essential for developing ethical guidelines and regulations that can effectively address the multifaceted ethical considerations of AI.

- Make ethical choices as consumers and users: Make conscious choices as consumers and users of AI technologies, supporting organisations and products that prioritise ethical AI practices. Choosing to support AI technologies that demonstrate ethical considerations can lead to a shift in the market, motivating competitors to follow suit and promoting a more responsible approach to AI. This ripple effect can lead to the creation of a safer, more inclusive AI ecosystem that safeguards user rights and societal well-being. As users, our preferences and behaviours shape AI's role in our daily lives. Utilizing platforms and applications that respect privacy, avoid biases, and uphold user rights reinforces the importance of ethical considerations. By demonstrating our preference for AI systems that prioritise ethical principles, we contribute to the development of technology that serves us responsibly and beneficially.

In conclusion, the active involvement of diverse stakeholders, including governments, organisations, and individuals, is an essential element for promoting ethical AI development and use. This collaborative effort is not merely beneficial but also vital in setting the course for how AI technologies are used and regulated.

Governments play a key role in this endeavour, particularly in establishing policy frameworks that guide the ethical use of AI. They have the power and responsibility to set regulations that ensure fairness, transparency, and accountability in AI systems, preventing misuse and harmful consequences. Governments can also promote AI literacy through educational policies, equipping citizens with the knowledge and skills to navigate an AI-driven world.

Organisations, both private and public, are at the forefront of AI development and implementation. As such, they have a significant responsibility to ensure their AI technologies align with ethical standards. This involves the adoption and implementation of ethical guidelines that go beyond mere legal compliance. Companies need to invest in research to identify and address potential ethical issues, continually updating their practices as AI technologies evolve.

Individuals, too, play a crucial role in this landscape. They must remain informed and engaged, advocating for ethical AI practices and holding organisations accountable. Public engagement in discussions and decisions around AI ethics ensures diverse perspectives are heard, contributing to a more inclusive and democratic approach to AI development.

All these efforts should converge towards a common goal: shaping a future where AI technologies not only contribute to societal advancement but also align with our moral principles. This ensures the creation of a more ethical, inclusive, and responsible society, one where AI serves humanity rather than subverts it.

In the following chapters, we will delve deeper into additional strategies for maintaining our humanity in the digital age. We'll discuss practical measures such as how to prepare for the future workforce, the importance of mental well-being, and how to effectively collaborate with AI, which are all essential components of our journey in an AI-driven world. Through these strategies, we can work towards a future where we not only effectively use AI but do so in a way that complements and enhances our shared human experience.

[206] https://www2.deloitte.com/content/dam/Deloitte/xe/Documents/About-Deloitte/WGS%20report%20I%20AI%20Ethics.pdf

[207] https://www.industry.gov.au/news/investments-grow-australias-critical-technologies-industries#:~:text=The%20government%20has%20committed%20%2441.2,AI%20governance%20and%20industry%20capability.

[208] https://www.gov.uk/government/news/54-million-boost-to-develop-secure-and-trustworthy-ai-research

[209] https://www.cnbc.com/2023/05/04/white-house-announces-ai-hub-investment.html

[210] https://www.sciencedirect.com/science/article/pii/S0740624X21000885

[211] https://www.linkedin.com/pulse/how-can-government-make-digital-services-more-inclusive-sear/

[212] https://www.reuters.com/sustainability/boards-policy-regulation/brandwatch-companies-woefully-behind-grappling-with-ethics-risks-ai-2023-06-13/

[213] https://www.forbes.com/sites/tomtaulli/2021/09/10/ai-artificial-intelligence-should-you-teach-it-to-your-employees/?sh=4c0314b77b73

[214] https://www.unite.ai/how-to-perform-an-ai-audit-in-2023/

[215] https://www.linkedin.com/advice/3/how-do-you-keep-up-latest-trends-innovations-7041842070671556608#:~:text=Follow%20online%20resources,and%20courses%20on%20AI%20topics.

[216] https://www.zdnet.com/article/what-technologists-can-do-to-promote-ai-ethics/

CHAPTER 8: AI AND THE FUTURE OF WORK

The Impact of AI on Jobs and Industries

The march of artificial intelligence (AI) continues unabated, permeating an expanding array of our daily experiences and increasingly asserting its influence on jobs and industries. The AI revolution heralds a new era, bringing with it a wave of transformations that reshape the contours of work, businesses, and entire industries. As AI grows more sophisticated, its impact reverberates across the economic landscape, stirring both trepidation and excitement. In this chapter, we delve into the profound ways AI is redefining the job market and various industries, shedding light on the emerging challenges and opportunities within this tech-infused reality.

AI's ability to learn, adapt, and execute tasks with unprecedented speed and accuracy has found utility across a diverse range of industries—from healthcare and education, to finance and insurance, to transportation and entertainment. However, as AI continues to evolve, it stirs fundamental questions about the future of work: Which jobs will AI augment? Which jobs will it displace? How do we prepare for an AI-infused future of work?

These concerns are coupled with immense opportunities. AI, with its transformative potential, is paving the way for new roles and industries that we are yet to envisage. As such, understanding these changes is crucial to ensure that we are well-equipped to adapt and thrive amidst this digital metamorphosis.

In this chapter, we aim to demystify the impact of AI on jobs and industries. We will delve into the specific ways AI is driving change—whether by enhancing efficiency, creating new roles, or displacing existing ones. By highlighting real-world examples from various industries, we will offer a comprehensive view of AI's transformative role. In addition, we will explore the challenges that come with these transformations, such as job displacement, privacy concerns, and the need for new skills.

Moreover, we will also emphasize the opportunities that AI ushers in—new jobs, enhanced decision-making, increased productivity, and the creation of innovative services and products. By mapping out potential strategies for individuals, businesses, and policymakers, we will provide practical guidance to help navigate this shifting landscape.

Join us on this exploration of the AI revolution's impact on jobs and industries as we investigate the intricacies of our changing world. As we peel back the layers of AI's influence, our aim is to equip you with a deep understanding, enabling you to seize opportunities, prepare for challenges, and navigate your path in the rapidly transforming world of work.

One of the most significant concerns regarding AI's impact on the job market is the potential displacement of jobs due to automation, particularly in sectors with high levels of routine, manual, and repetitive tasks. Some key aspects of job displacement and automation include the following:

- Automation of routine tasks: AI technologies have the potential to automate many routine tasks, leading to job displacement in industries that rely heavily on manual and repetitive labour. Automation also creates innovation, which will lead to new types of jobs. However, office administrative support, legal, architecture and engineering, business and financial operations, management, sales, healthcare, and art and design are some industries and sectors that will be impacted by automation. It is believed that over 50 million Chinese workers will require retraining as a result of AI deployment. The US will need to reskill 11.5 million people in order for them to remain employable. Millions across Brazil, Japan, and Europe will also need help as AI and related technologies permeate the workforce. Routine tasks are where AI will make huge inroads positively, cutting costs for businesses but at the cost of human workers such as checkout operators in supermarkets, toll collectors, fast-food service staff, and even paralegals. AI has the potential to impact a lot more areas of the workforce, whether through direct job replacement, wage loss, or even a rise in income inequality. [217]

- Effects on low-skilled and middle-skilled jobs: Low-skilled and middle-skilled jobs are often considered to be at higher risk of displacement due to automation, as these roles typically involve tasks that can be easily automated. In middle and low-skilled jobs, AI systems will complete the easily automated tasks while humans continue to perform those that cannot yet be automated. There is a high probability that the increase in automation through AI will deliver and create new tasks and jobs; however, these jobs and tasks are likely to be highly skilled. This is a concern, as AI will only continue to exacerbate the divide between the tech haves and have-nots. Technology will keep the poor poor while the rich get even richer. Again, this is where reskilling and retraining entire workforces needs to become a priority for companies and governments to ensure no one is left behind as technology continues to evolve and affect the labour force. [218]

- Regional and demographic disparities: Job displacement due to automation may disproportionately affect certain regions and demographic groups, exacerbating existing social and economic inequalities. There is already a digital divide visible in any well-developed country. On one hand you have the digitally orientated metropolitan areas, and on the other, the lower-tech smaller cities, towns, and rural areas. The link between AI and geography is likely to follow past technology diffusion, such as the personal computers where the cities that adopted PCs earliest and fastest saw their relative wages increase the quickest. The government could support bottom-up local solutions and incentivise regions to align their education, workforce, and training as well as their economic development with one another along with employers' needs and the new importance of AI-related tech skills. Essentially, we should be accelerating the adoption of new technologies by our regional economies to help them become more resilient. As the IT era transforms into the AI era, what will the next phase of interplay between automation and employment look like? [219]

While AI has the potential to displace certain jobs, it also creates opportunities for new jobs, industries, and skill sets. Some key aspects of the emergence of new job opportunities and industries include the following:

- New roles in AI-related fields: As AI technologies continue to advance, new roles will emerge in AI-related fields, such as data science, machine learning engineering, and AI ethics. As the AI industry matures, jobs in AI-related fields will not only grow in number but also complexity and diversity. Whilst AI is not new, we explored its history very early on in this book, and it is now undergoing a rapid growth period as new breakthroughs are made what seems like daily. Not all careers in artificial intelligence are similar though. There are various kinds of jobs, all of which require quite specific skills. Software engineers, software architects, big data specialists, and natural language processing engineers, to name a few. My favourite, as I'm always interested in how companies manage data and insights, is a business intelligence developer. This role processes complex internal and external data to identify trends. Business intelligence developers are not like data analysts because they don't create the reports themselves. They are generally responsible for designing, modelling and maintaining complex data in cloud-based platforms for business users to view through highly engaging dashboards. [220]

- The rise of complementary jobs: The integration of AI technologies in various industries can lead to the creation of complementary jobs that support and enhance the capabilities of AI systems. Here are a few examples of jobs we could see in the future:

  - AI trainers and operators: These professionals will use and train AI systems and fine-tune them to achieve expected outcomes.

  - Sentiment analyser: Someone who can use generative AI to interpret blog posts, ratings, and reviews, etc. to understand customer sentiments using their understanding of human emotion and context.

  - Prompt engineer: This role has already emerged as generative AI hit the mainstream. It focuses on writing text and not code. Prompt engineers need to understand natural language processing and be able to optimise prompts to improve the outcome of large language models.

- AI integration specialists. Organisations will look to these specialists for assistance in adopting and implementing AI into their business operations. These specialists will have to understand company-specific workflows and be able to identify areas that could benefit from AI and customise solutions to suit. [221]
- Reshaping existing industries: AI has the potential to revolutionize existing industries, such as healthcare, transportation, and agriculture, creating new job opportunities and transforming the way work is performed within these sectors. It is not just white-collar workers in offices who will see their day-to-day work change. More traditional manual labour–based industries are already implementing AI into their work lives. Farmers are using AI to collect data on resource consumption to forecast crop production and detect crop diseases. Logistics centres are using AI to help determine which vehicles to choose based on load, which route to take, how to pack and sort packages, and even where to locate distribution centres. Even athletes aren't impervious to AI. Analysing video recordings of matches is nothing new, but these video files can be augmented with object detection and pose elimination technology. This means coaches can gather information about players and extract hidden patterns from numerous games. [222]

As AI continues to transform the job market, it is crucial to invest in reskilling and upskilling programs that help workers adapt to the changing landscape. Key aspects of reskilling and upskilling in the age of AI include the following:

- Lifelong learning: Embracing a lifelong learning mindset is essential for individuals to stay relevant and competitive in the job market as AI technologies continue to advance.
- Development of transferable skills: Focusing on the development of transferable skills, such as critical thinking, problem-solving, and communication, can help workers adapt to new roles and industries that emerge as a result of AI-driven transformations.
- Government and organizational support: Governments and organisations play a crucial role in providing support for reskilling and upskilling initiatives, ensuring that workers have access to the resources and opportunities needed to adapt to the changing job market.

In conclusion, the influence of artificial intelligence on the job market and industries is a multifaceted landscape that brings forth a blend of challenges and promising opportunities. The concern of job displacement due to automation is undeniably substantial, yet it's equally important to recognise that AI has the potential to reshape industries and cultivate new avenues for employment, thereby offering society a broader spectrum of benefits.

The apprehensions surrounding job displacement are not unfounded, as automation and AI-driven advancements continue to redefine traditional roles and tasks. However, it's imperative to approach this transformation as an impetus for change rather than an insurmountable hurdle. The dynamic nature of AI provides the groundwork for innovation, enabling industries to evolve and adapt to the demands of the digital age.

In this transformative environment, fostering a lifelong learning mindset emerges as a pivotal strategy. Embracing continuous learning is not merely a response to the shifts brought about by AI but a proactive approach to personal and professional development. By investing in reskilling and upskilling initiatives, individuals can effectively realign their skills with the emerging needs of industries. This strategic approach empowers workers to not only weather the storm of automation but also to harness its potential for their benefit.

Furthermore, AI's transformative power can't be underestimated in terms of job creation. As traditional roles evolve, new opportunities emerge, requiring a diverse set of skills ranging from AI-related expertise to soft skills that remain quintessentially human. Embracing these new roles and leveraging the symbiotic relationship between AI and human capabilities will be the cornerstone of thriving in the age of AI.

By blending the best of human ingenuity with AI's capabilities, individuals and organisations can seize the array of opportunities that AI introduces. Through resolute efforts to adapt, learn, and evolve, the workforce can pave the way for a more agile and responsive job market that leverages the power of AI to enhance productivity, innovation, and economic growth.

[217] https://www.forbes.com/sites/jackkelly/2023/03/31/goldman-sachs-predicts-300-million-jobs-will-be-lost-or-degraded-by-artificial-intelligence/?sh=40a62a0d782b

[218] https://www.bruegel.org/blog-post/artificial-intelligences-great-impact-low-and-middle-skilled-jobs

[219] https://www.brookings.edu/articles/countering-the-geographical-impacts-of-automation-computers-ai-and-place-disparities/

[220] https://www.brookings.edu/articles/countering-the-geographical-impacts-of-automation-computers-ai-and-place-disparities/

[221] https://www.forbes.com/sites/forbestechcouncil/2023/07/06/20-new-and-enhanced-roles-ai-could-create/?sh=6726e65d6f04

[222] https://www.imaginarycloud.com/blog/how-artificial-intelligence-is-transforming-every-industry-2/

How to Prepare for the Future Workforce

In an era where artificial intelligence is an ever-present force shaping the job market and industries, the imperative to proactively prepare for the future workforce has never been more pronounced. This chapter delves into a comprehensive exploration of strategies and approaches aimed at not only navigating but thriving within the evolving landscape of work, underpinned by the transformative potential of AI.

As AI-driven technologies weave their way into every facet of industries, from manufacturing to finance and beyond, the notion of traditional job roles undergoes a paradigm shift. With this transformation in mind, it's imperative for individuals, organisations, and governments to adopt a forward-thinking stance that revolves around adaptability and strategic alignment.

The individual level bears the responsibility of embracing a proactive stance towards continuous learning and skills enhancement. Through reskilling and upskilling initiatives, individuals can both realign their existing skill sets and cultivate novel proficiencies that are aligned with the emerging needs of the AI-driven job market. By nurturing a growth mindset and embracing lifelong learning, workers are positioned to become versatile, agile contributors capable of embracing new roles and challenges.

On the organizational front, adaptation becomes a cornerstone of sustained success. Enterprises that grasp the potential of AI-driven advancements and strategically integrate them into their operations stand to unlock unprecedented efficiencies and innovation. However, this also necessitates a holistic approach to workforce management, including the creation of a conducive environment for continuous learning and skill development.

Governments, in their capacity as key regulators and facilitators, must play a pivotal role in facilitating this transition. The formulation of policies that encourage reskilling and upskilling programs, incentivize research and development in AI-related fields, and ensure equitable access to opportunities in the AI-driven job market is paramount. By fostering an ecosystem that nurtures the growth of AI while safeguarding the interests of the workforce, governments can contribute to a harmonious coexistence between AI-driven technological progress and the workforce.

This chapter offers an intricate exploration of these strategies and approaches, carving a path that guides individuals, organisations, and governments towards a future workforce primed to navigate the dynamic AI-driven landscape. By embracing these insights and incorporating them into practices, the aim is to transcend the challenges and seize the opportunities that AI's transformative influence holds, ultimately fostering an environment where humans and AI converge to drive a prosperous and progressive society.

Emotional intelligence and human skills, such as empathy, intuition, and understanding of emotions, will become increasingly valuable in the age of AI. These skills can help do the following:

- Soft Skills: In the early years of the twenty-first century, there has been a marked shift in the re-importance people and certainly employers are placing on soft skills. Soft skills, or as they are more commonly known, *people skills*, are a set of personal attributes that enable you to interact effectively with others. While there is a growing demand for technical skills in the age of AI, these tech-based skills are not enough to succeed in the modern workplace. Soft skills can't be replicated by AI. Machines can't replicate empathy, creativity, or critical thinking. Soft skills also complement technical skills. Soft skills are also essential for leadership. As companies continue to adopt new technologies, leadership skills become crucial. Leaders with well-developed soft skills can build and maintain strong relationships, foster collaboration, and inspire people to achieve their potential. [223]
- Facilitate decision-making: Balancing emotional intelligence with AI-driven data analysis can lead to better decision-making that considers both objective data and human values. AI can provide insights into data that humans may not be able to easily see or simply take too long to process. By analysing this data and finding patterns, AI can help inform humans when trying to make personal or business decisions. A future where humans work alongside AI and harness it to make better-informed decisions faster and with more clarity is surely the future we will see come to fruition. It can't be underestimated; while we will see job displacement, there are simply some parts of being human that AI simply can't do. There will be a need for humans to do a lot of work in the future; some of this will leverage AI, and some will not. Humans will still need to oversee and make final decisions in a lot of industries. [224]
- Support customer service and human-centric roles: Human skills will remain essential in roles that require a deep understanding of human emotions and needs, such as customer service, healthcare, and education. AI is not sophisticated enough to understand cultural differences in expressing and reading emotions, making it hard for AI to draw accurate conclusions. This could result in emotional bias, which can perpetuate stereotypes and assumptions at an unprecedented scale. If you have ever been on hold with any government service or even large phone company here in Australia, you likely have been asked, "In a few words, please tell me the reason for your call today", by a human yet technology-driven voice. More often than not, the AI chatbot gets your statement wrong and transfers you to the wrong department. By the time you finally speak to a human, you are often frustrated and still not able to find a solution to the problem that required you to call in the first place. This is where humans in customer service roles will still be important and

very much a human-centric role. The humans in these roles should use AI to make the process more efficient. [225]

Preparing for the future workforce involves investing in education and training programs that do the following:

- Promote digital literacy: Ensuring that individuals possess basic digital skills is crucial for navigating the increasingly technology-driven job market. Disruptive innovation has changed human lives before. The printing press drove up linguistic rates, upended entrenched political and social structures, and opened up a world of knowledge to the masses. Digital literacy means having the skills you need to live, learn, and work in a society where communication and access to information is increasingly via digital technologies such as the internet, social media, and mobile devices and increasingly powered by AI. We need to start thinking about how we embed these skills into our social practices and take care of minorities or groups of people who need assistance making the shift to this way of life. Much like Covid accelerated some economies further towards a cashless society, many older people are struggling with this, as they don't know how to use mobile banking. When AI implementation really starts to integrate into our daily lives, these people need to not be forgotten. Digital literacy is a long-term investment; it's about helping citizens navigate their lives. AI will only become more accurate and less detectable. Governments really need to start investing in digital literacy programs and policies to ensure society moves forwards together. [226]

- Encourage lifelong learning: Cultivating a culture of lifelong learning will enable individuals to adapt to new roles and industries that emerge as AI technologies advance. The world is continuing to change at a very fast pace. Technologies such as AI will only increase that pace. To keep up and be prepared for the future workforce, embracing lifelong learning will give you the capability to remain successful in your current role or even pivot into new roles. Challenges stimulate learning and growth and bring a sense of fulfillment. Challenges and difficulties are what force us to grow. Pair these feelings with opportunities to learn, and you will find yourself with a growth mindset and looking for future opportunities to grow and learn. A willingness to take calculated risks will also help position you strongly for a future workforce that looks set to change as technology keeps evolving. [227]

- Provide reskilling and upskilling opportunities: Governments and organisations should support reskilling and upskilling programs that help workers acquire new skills and knowledge in response to the changing job market. As we have outlined numerous times, advances in technology are changing the demand for skills at an accelerated pace. AI can handle a growing number of repetitive and manual-based tasks as well as perform increasingly sophisticated knowledge work such as research, coding, and writing. These have long been thought of as safe from the reaches of automation or at least tech-based disruption. Upskilling, whilst noble, may not be enough. Reskilling will be required, which will be a quite complex societal challenge that will require some of us to not only acquire new skills but also to use those skills to change occupations. During times of disruption, people and companies often turn to reskilling to soften the blow of redundancies. In the face of AI advances, reskilling and upskilling are now strategic imperatives. In the future, reskilling and upskilling employees should be a core part of a business's core value proposition to their staff, where they promote and build time into the workweek for employees to pursue new skills. Whilst people should make reskilling and upskilling their own priority, governments and companies must make them a focus in the future as we are still getting a grasp on what impact AI will have on the very near future job market and labour force. [228]

Effective collaboration between stakeholders, including governments, organisations, educational institutions, and individuals, is essential for preparing the future workforce. This collaboration can involve the following:

- Developing policy frameworks and strategies: Governments should work with other stakeholders to develop comprehensive policy frameworks and strategies that address the challenges and opportunities presented by AI, for example, *job polarisation*, which is the division in the labour market between high-paid, high-skilled jobs and low-paid, low-skilled jobs with a decline in middle-skilled and middle-paid positions. Inclusive policies and support structures are essential to equitably distribute the benefits of AI. This is why it is crucial governments, businesses, education institutes, and society at large collaborate to create a future of work that everyone can access. [229]
- Sharing resources and expertise: Organisations and educational institutions can collaborate to share resources, expertise, and best practices in preparing the future workforce for the age of AI. A skills-based approach helps both employers and employees. Skills-based practices are a powerful solution to the challenges we are starting to face in a tech-driven world. Education institutes need to interface with industry more closely to understand what skills students require when they are preparing them in the classroom for the real world. Businesses often have to spend a lot of money and time in training employees fresh to their industry, and this will always be the case. However, if businesses and the education industry share their resources and partner on a deeper level, we can close this gap. Consider having business experts go and teach a few days a semester online or in person to share with students what they should expect in the professional world. Student work-experience days, interviews, and collaborations between businesses and the education sector could all help better prepare our younger generations for what to expect when they join the workforce, just how they can use their skills, and what they will continue to learn on the job. [230]
- Engaging the public: Public engagement and dialogue on AI and the future of work can help raise awareness, inform policymaking, and ensure

that diverse perspectives are considered. As the saying goes—be alert not alarmed. Public engagement would almost definitely improve AI research, as most AI researchers are male and are likely to be from wealthy backgrounds. The theories behind collective intelligence and cognitive diversity show that more diverse groups are better at solving problems. Because AI will have such wide-ranging effects, I believe it's in everyone's personal best interests to engage with it, learn more about it, and, if you can, try to have an impact on its future direction. Currently, only a tiny group of people are making hugely important decisions that have far-reaching and as yet somewhat unknown consequences. [231]

In the relentless march towards an AI-imbued future, the preparation of our workforce assumes a central role in shaping the trajectory of this transformation. In the face of evolving landscapes and redefined paradigms, the culmination of our efforts is encapsulated in a dynamic conclusion that underscores the multi-faceted approach essential for the journey ahead.

As the contours of industry and employment undergo profound reconfiguration, the imperative for adaptability takes centre stage. The resonance of traditional skill sets is reshaped by the demands of AI, urging individuals and organisations to cultivate an unwavering willingness to learn, unlearn, and relearn. This adaptability, fuelled by an inherent growth mindset, empowers the workforce to seamlessly transition between roles and domains, harnessing the evolving AI landscape to their advantage.

Yet, this transformation isn't solely defined by technical proficiency. The linchpin of emotional intelligence and human skills also emerges as pivotal. These qualities, deeply ingrained in our humanity, enrich our ability to interact, empathize, and collaborate. Within an AI-dominated world, these human nuances stand as a testament to the indispensable role of human insight and connection, underscoring the irreplaceable value of our emotional depth.

In fostering a workforce prepared for the AI frontier, investing in education and training programs emerges as an essential requirement. These initiatives, thoughtfully designed to blend theoretical foundations with practical applications, empower individuals with the acumen to traverse the complexities of AI integration. By fortifying this educational infrastructure, we cultivate a pipeline of talent poised to tackle the challenges and innovate within the realm of AI.

However, this collective journey cannot be embarked upon in isolation. Collaboration among stakeholders forms the nucleus of an enriched AI workforce. Governments, organisations, educational institutions, and individuals must synergize their efforts, sharing insights, best practices, and resources to craft a cohesive and comprehensive approach. By converging strengths and perspectives, this collaborative front creates a fortified framework that bridges the chasm between technological evolution and human excellence.

In traversing the multifaceted dimensions of preparing the future workforce for an AI-driven epoch, the amalgamation of these strategies and approaches becomes our lodestar. This coalescence ensures that our workforce stands as a testament to the harmonious interplay between human ingenuity and technological progress. As the digital age dawns, this concerted effort to bridge the realms of AI and humanity acts as the catalyst, propelling us towards an era where innovation thrives and the human essence remains firmly intact.

[223] https://www.linkedin.com/pulse/age-ai-soft-skills-shine-ashish-gupta#:~:text=As%20organisations%20adopt%20new%20technologies,are%20essential%20for%20effective%20leadership.

[224] https://enterprisersproject.com/article/2023/4/ai-decision-making

[225] https://www.linkedin.com/pulse/age-ai-soft-skills-shine-ashish-gupta#:~:text=As%20organisations%20adopt%20new%20technologies,are%20essential%20for%20effective%20leadership.

[226] https://srinstitute.utoronto.ca/news/digital-literacy-will-be-key-in-a-world-transformed-by-ai

[227] https://www.forbes.com/sites/forbeshumanresourcescouncil/2021/09/30/embrace-lifelong-learning-to-thrive-in-the-future-of-work/?sh=5b1a66a37631

[228] https://hbr.org/2023/09/reskilling-in-the-age-of-ai

[229] https://www.techopedia.com/the-future-of-work-in-the-age-of-ai

[230] https://www.mckinsey.com/capabilities/people-and-organizational-performance/our-insights/taking-a-skills-based-approach-to-building-the-future-workforce

[231] https://www.nesta.org.uk/blog/how-to-involve-the-public-in-the-development-of-artificial-intelligence/

Collaborating with AI to Enhance Human Potential

The uncharted territory we navigate holds the promise of a profound transformation. At the heart of this metamorphosis is the imperative to cultivate a symbiotic partnership between AI and human ingenuity.

In this section, we'll dive into the ways in which humans could use AI to supercharge our day to day lives to define a new era of collaboration. The potential of AI interlaced into humans' day to day lives is what has captured attention over the last 18 months as social commentators start to think of AI not as Artificial Intelligence but as *Augmented Intelligence* where humans using AI are faster, more efficient, happier, and healthier in their day to day lives as a result of leveraging this technology. This partnership does not diminish human contribution; rather, it amplifies human capabilities by augmenting our strengths.

This collaborative narrative illuminates the pathway to a more productive and gratifying work existence. The synergy between humans and AI unlocks doors to heightened efficiency, enabling us to accomplish tasks that once lingered in the realm of the unattainable. Amid this coexistence, the productivity gains are sure to unlock further innovation as humans are freed to think more creatively and innovate more than ever before.

Yet, at the heart of this partnership lies a profound truth: ethics and humanity are the inspirations that guide our journey. The chapter underscores the importance of crafting AI partnerships founded on ethical considerations. This blueprint ensures that while machines augment our abilities, human values remain at the forefront, safeguarding our distinct identity and anchoring us in a shared moral compass.

In sum, the chapter's exploration delivers a vision of collaboration where human ingenuity works hand-in-hand with AI innovation. Together, they deliver an environment where potential is no longer confined to singular capability but amplified by a harmonic alliance. This vision pushes us to explore a future where human creativity and AI's computational prowess resonates as a unified fusion of progress and purpose.

Human-AI collaboration involves leveraging the unique strengths of both humans and AI systems to achieve optimal outcomes. Some key aspects of human-AI collaboration include the following:

- Enhancing human creativity: AI can be used as a creative tool, generating ideas and possibilities that humans can refine and build upon, leading to novel and innovative solutions. One of the early examples of AI was when IBM's Deep Blue beat chess grandmaster Gary Kasparov in 1997. Many people actually feared that humans would begin to abandon the game and pursuit of chess mastery because they would "never be as good as a computer". In actual fact, the opposite happened. There was widespread adoption of computer simulations, which made humans better. AI will not come up with our best ideas for us. It will, however, greatly reduce the cost, time, and effort of generating new ideas. It will set our creativity free rather than replace it. It will give us superpowers by empowering us to broadly explore a vast range of knowledge from many different domains and could help us deliver even greater innovation throughout society. Brainstorming with various AI platforms is something I have tried, and as someone who counts themselves amongst the self-confessed non-creative types, these platforms really help me get ideas out of my head as I learn to direct AI platforms and get them to work my ideas out with me. [232]

- Collaborative problem-solving: Combining human expertise and AI capabilities can lead to more effective problem-solving, as humans and AI systems can contribute different perspectives and approaches to address complex challenges. AI won't replace us; it will augment us. Never before have digital tools been so responsive to us nor we to them. Research has shown that when humans and machines work together, we see the greatest performance improvements. Human qualities and strengths such as leadership, teamwork, creativity, and social skills paired with AI skills such as speed, scalability, and quantitative capabilities will only lead to deeper collaboration with our machines and deliver much better problem-solving capabilities. [233]

To effectively collaborate with AI systems, individuals must develop a mindset that embraces the potential of AI while acknowledging its limitations. Key aspects of cultivating a mindset for human-AI collaboration include the following:

- Recognising the value of AI: Individuals should appreciate the potential of AI to enhance productivity, creativity, and decision-making, viewing AI as a valuable tool rather than a threat. If you dive into the AI world and start exploring different platforms, you will quickly see that AI won't replace you but will augment you with superpowers. You could be asking Chat GPT for fifty ways to use a toothpick, creating artistic imagery with Midjourney, or elevating your search workflows with Perplexity. The latest generative AI platform releases are very compelling because almost anyone can use them. As we've touched on several times throughout this book, generative AI tools have the ability to take almost all the mundane and repetitive task-based work off humans and free us to work on higher-value tasks. Generative AI is a tool, not a threat, and it's about using the tool at the right time for the right job. [234]
- Acknowledging AI limitations: It is essential to understand the limitations of AI systems, such as their inability to fully replicate human emotions, intuition, and complex reasoning. For all the amazing content today's modern generative AI can produce, it still has limitations. As with any new technology, it is always helpful to take a step back and assess the strengths and weaknesses in order to better focus our research efforts and uses of such platforms moving forward. Humans have common sense, which is a consequence of the fact that we develop persistent mental representations of people, places, and other concepts around our

world. Neural networks can't form these sorts of connections or mental models. They don't possess discrete, grounded representations of the human world or the people and objects in our world. They merely rely on statistical relationships within data to generate insights that aren't always accurate. For example, when asked what is heavier, a toaster or a pencil? Chat GPT responded that a pencil was heavier. Humans possess mental models of both those objects; we can picture them and their shape, size, and weight. In contrast, Chat GPT relies on statistical patterns captured from its training data. The absence of common sense prevents AI systems like this from understanding the world and communicating naturally. It's worth keeping this in mind when the inevitable "AI will replace us all" pundits come out of the woodwork. Humans are still far more intelligent than AI platforms. [235]

- Emphasizing human skills and values: A collaborative mindset involves recognising the unique skills and values that humans possess, such as empathy, creativity, and ethical decision-making. We need to recognise these skills are what humans and only humans can bring to the table. However these are not innate talents and therefore need to be developed through practice and dedication. Everyone has unique abilities worth nurturing, so if we focus on bringing those to the fore, we could find innovation in places and people where we have never looked before. AI will get better at being AI and doing what it does. Humans should then focus on getting better as humans and growing and developing the unique skills they have to remain successful in the age of AI. [236]

Organisations play a crucial role in fostering human-AI collaboration by creating work environments that support and encourage collaboration between humans and AI systems. Some key strategies for developing collaborative work environments include the following:

- Integrating AI into workflows: Organisations should actively integrate AI systems into existing workflows, allowing humans and AI to work together seamlessly and effectively. Similar to any other technology implementation, embedding AI into your workflows is not that different. To successfully implement AI, I would suggest identifying your goals. What do you want to achieve by implementing AI? Are you looking for efficiency gains, improved accuracy? Next, analyse your current workflows. Is it time-consuming, could it be automated, is AI the right solution, and what could go wrong? Now move on to selecting the right AI solution. Factors to consider here are obviously cost and scalability. If your business or customer base grows, will your AI solution be able to handle that? Ease of use is a huge one; a good UI/UX is critical to success. Finally, is the AI solution compatible with your existing systems—can it be integrated easily? The fourth step is to implement the solution. Communicate the implementation plan with all relevant stakeholders. Test and iterate, as problems will likely arise in this part of the project. Lastly, monitor performance to ensure your new workflow with its embedded AI is meeting its objectives. If there are issues with speed, accuracy, or user satisfaction, you can then optimise these parts over time. [237]

- Providing training and resources: Organisations should offer training and resources to help employees develop the skills and knowledge necessary to work effectively with AI systems. Try to avoid making any training too heavy on technical talk and jargon where possible. Nothing will get your colleagues' eyes glazing over quicker than deep diving into deep learning, feedback loops, and generative adversarial networks. If you can, make training hands-on. As someone who has spent a large part of their career training people on technology, I always find hands-on training is absorbed quicker than any video, manual, or lecture. Make sure you keep your training up to date. This can be a bit frustrating, given the speed at which AI platforms are being released or even just updated. Collect feedback from training participants to help you refine your content and delivery for future sessions. [238]

- Encouraging a culture of collaboration: Organisations should promote a culture that values collaboration, innovation, and adaptability, encouraging employees to embrace human-AI collaboration as a means to achieve shared goals. Promote a supportive work environment and encourage your teams to collaborate using the latest technology. Impress upon your team the importance of developing AI literacy and facilitating a culture that embraces change, innovation, and continuous learning. Developing and promoting a symbiotic relationship with AI in your workplace could help enhance productivity overall, improve decision-making, and promote the well-being of your staff. If you push staff to engage with these platforms, it's likely they will find better ways of working, collaborating, and engaging day to day with their work and each other. The draconian bans on generative AI in the workplace will only serve to undermine staff sentiment and the feeling that they aren't trusted, which will only breed a negative culture. [239]

As humans and AI systems collaborate more closely, it is crucial to navigate the ethical considerations that arise, such as ensuring fairness, accountability, and transparency in AI-driven decision-making. Some key aspects of navigating ethical considerations in human-AI collaboration include the following:

- Encouraging ethical awareness: Organisations should foster an environment where employees are encouraged to consider the ethical implications of their work with AI systems and make responsible decisions accordingly. I think policies and guidelines are good places to start if the company backs them up and enforces them. A use of generative AI policy or ethical uses of AI guidelines help staff and businesses understand that ethical awareness starts with careful forethought to ensure your actions are ethically sound. It signals to the business and its employees that there is thought going into the long- and short-term effects generative AI will have on employees, customers, and business relationships, not to mention the work being produced. Whilst most people believe behaving ethically is its own reward, for businesses, it is likely to have financial rewards too. Unethical actions could result in brand and reputation damage, jeopardising relationships with suppliers and partners as well as causing public relationship problems. Encouraging ethical behaviour and detailing ethical guidelines will help decrease unethical behaviour and increase awareness. At the very least, if someone does accidentally or maliciously act unethically, you can educate them on the companies' guidelines to avoid repeat behaviour. [240]

- Establishing guidelines and oversight: Organisations should implement guidelines and oversight mechanisms to monitor and evaluate the ethical implications of human-AI collaboration, proactively addressing any concerns or issues that arise. You won't be able to devise ethic-based procedures for every possible situation, so employees will need some form of guidance and ethical oversight for unexpected situations. [241]

At its core, the essence of collaborating with AI to enhance human potential lies in the delicate fusion of their distinctive strengths. The analytical prowess of AI systems, adept at sifting through colossal datasets, converges with the nuanced creativity of human minds, forging an alliance that transforms information into insights. This synergy transforms the landscape, creating a seamless experience where the outputs are more than the sum of their individual components.

In this transformative journey, a mindset shift becomes the cornerstone. It involves embracing AI not as a rival but as a catalyst that amplifies human capabilities. This shift catalyses a journey of exploration, allowing individuals and organisations to harness AI's capacities as instruments of empowerment rather than sources of trepidation. It opens the door to a universe of possibilities, where AI becomes a co-pilot on the voyage of innovation.

Amid this evolution of coworking with AI and augmenting our daily lives and tasks, ethical considerations emerge as important principles. As the realms of ethics and technology intertwine, a robust framework emerges—one that upholds the dignity of human values while fostering innovation. By thoughtfully delineating boundaries and ensuring that ethical considerations underscore every partnership, a sustainable, harmonious coexistence takes root.

[232] https://time.com/6289278/ai-affect-human-creativity/

[233] https://hbr.org/2018/07/collaborative-intelligence-humans-and-ai-are-joining-forces

[234] https://www.mckinsey.com/about-us/new-at-mckinsey-blog/generative-ai-can-give-you-superpowers-new-mckinsey-research-finds

[235] https://www.mckinsey.com/about-us/new-at-mckinsey-blog/generative-ai-can-give-you-superpowers-new-mckinsey-research-finds

[236] https://www.hrzone.com/talent/development/six-essential-human-skills-to-stay-competitive-in-the-age-of-ai

[237] https://www.bairesdev.com/blog/a-guide-to-inserting-ai-into-your-workflow/

[238] https://www.bairesdev.com/blog/a-guide-to-inserting-ai-into-your-workflow/

[239] https://www.forbes.com/sites/forbesbusinesscouncil/2023/07/26/the-human-ai-symbiosis-embracing-collaboration-for-a-smarter-future/?sh=4e4b4cc256b6

[240] https://smallbusiness.chron.com/ethical-awareness-business-24273.html

[241] https://smallbusiness.chron.com/incorporate-ethics-work-26131.html

CHAPTER 9: MINDFULNESS AND MENTAL HEALTH

The Importance of Mental Well-Being in a Digital World

As the age of artificial intelligence and digital technology matures, its grip on our lives intensifies. Technology's ubiquitous nature has streamlined many facets of our existence, augmenting our capabilities and offering a wealth of conveniences. However, amid the rapid digital transformation, it is crucial not to overlook the importance of mental well-being and mindfulness. In this section, we will delve into the pressing need for mental well-being in the digital age, spotlight the benefits of mindfulness, and share effective strategies for cultivating mental wellness.

Living in a world where screens demand our attention and AI increasingly mediates our experiences, the pressures on mental health are mounting. From the stress of relentless connectivity to the anxiety induced by the pace of AI-driven changes, these challenges are part and parcel of our digital existence. Hence, it becomes paramount to acknowledge these pressures, understand their implications, and take proactive measures to safeguard our mental well-being.

At the heart of this mental well-being lies the practice of mindfulness. An ancient technique finding new relevance in our digital world, mindfulness invites us to inhabit the present moment fully, to experience it without judgement or distraction. Amid the constant buzz of notifications and the ceaseless influx of information, mindfulness offers a much-needed respite, a sanctuary where our humanity can breathe, unfettered by digital demands.

In this chapter, we will explore how these practices can enhance emotional resilience, improve focus, and lead to greater self-awareness—qualities that fortify us against the pressures of our digital lives. We will also discuss the scientific underpinnings of mindfulness, linking its practice to improved mental health outcomes and increased overall well-being.

This chapter will provide actionable insights to cultivate mindfulness and mental well-being in your everyday life. From incorporating mindfulness exercises into your daily routine to leveraging technology itself in service of mental health, we will provide an array of tools to support your journey towards mental wellness and cultivate a mindful approach to technology.

The rapid advancement of AI and digital technologies has brought about new challenges for mental health, such as the following:

- Information overload: The constant flow of information and the pressure to stay connected can lead to stress, anxiety, and burnout. There's a lot to unpack here. Information overload is also known as *infobesity*, *infoxication*, and *information anxiety*. Information overload is difficulty understanding an issue and making effective decisions when one has too much information about the issue. It is mostly associated with the excessive quantity of daily information. The advent of modern technology has been the primary driver of information overload on multiple fronts—quantity produced, ease of dissemination, and breadth of audience reached. The cost of information overload is that people get distracted and make more errors due to attempts to multitask, and as a result, they accomplish less, and large priorities fall by the wayside in lieu of attention-grabbing tasks. If we think about our own role in information overload, you could say it's a consequence of a deeper problem—filter failure. This is where humans continue to overshare information with each other, with the rapid rise of social media apps and wireless access and connectivity. Remember when Instagram first came out and people started taking photos of their food? Prior to social media, we had to share this sort of information in an analog environment. In the case of food pictures, you would generally share that meal with whoever joined you at the restaurant or tell your friends about a great new restaurant you tried out recently. With social media, we could instantly see where people were, who they were with, and what their political and religious views were, and the majority of us uploaded this information willingly to these huge websites. No wonder we are overloaded. In a few short years we moved from digesting media to being the prime creators with every post, tweet, and status update. [242]

- Digital addiction: The addictive nature of digital devices and social media can contribute to feelings of isolation, loneliness, and decreased life satisfaction. There has been so much research in this area over the past couple of years. I wrote about it earlier in this book that we took years to work out how bad social media was for people and that we need to be careful how AI is developed, as the true consequences on humans mentally are unknown. The chemical reaction we have to these technologies is creating digital addictions. It's now well understood that dopamine, the chemical released in the brain that makes us feel good, and the hyper-social environments provided through our smartphones are intertwined, and the social media and technology giants are all too aware of this. Smartphones and social media are what we turn to for a quick hit of dopamine, with each swipe, like, and tweet. Since the turn of the millennium, behavioural addictions have skyrocketed. Our lives are tech soaked. You leave your office having stared at a laptop screen all day only to stare at your smartphone screen on the way home, followed by some more TV screen at home, etc. According to a World Happiness Report, depression rates are climbing, and people in high-income countries have become more unhappy. We have forgotten how to be alone with our thoughts and rarely concentrate on large tasks or get into creative flow states. The more and more engrossed we become in our digital devices, the more and more we can become unsatisfied with our own lives, which leads to anxiety and depression. As AI starts to permeate our lives even further, one has to wonder, if we already experience these issues with our smartphones, will AI supercharge these feelings of loneliness, isolation, and depression?... [243]

- The impact on work-life balance: The increasingly blurred lines between work and personal life, exacerbated by remote work arrangements, can negatively affect mental well-being. Working remotely during the pandemic was not even a choice. The flexibility that working remotely delivered has now become the norm. However, the continued blurred lines between work and home beyond the pandemic have increased employee stress and diminished overall well-being. Personal life alone has many competing priorities, such as balancing friendships, relationships, childcare limitations and education, and just general household duties. When also trying to work in a remote environment around these other priorities, it can induce stress and negative mental health. It can already be difficult enough to turn off after a day working in the office, as we are still connected via our devices. That connection, for some, can be harder to break when working from home and trying to extricate yourself from your computer and work at a reasonable time. This boundary has become blurred as work has entered our personal space. Our home space away from the office is now also an office, and we all have a responsibility to ourselves to set boundaries and protect our mental health. A balanced workplace culture is also critical to ensure employees feel comfortable and supported in their life outside of the workplace. Employers aren't and should be responsible for everything, though the circumstances of the pandemic somewhat normalised an overlap between work and life. We need to return this balance to a clearer separation of work and home life. Flexibility is key for employers and employees to keep in mind. We must remember in this new age of work, with increasing technology options keeping us tethered to work and colleagues, that things like flexible hours, agile work options, and support for non-work (typically family-based) priorities and obligations won't distract staff but actually engage them more to do their best work at the times of day that suit them. I'm by no means promoting that everyone should work wherever and whenever, but flexibility and trust in employees will bring out the best in them, and the business will benefit. Technology only exacerbates the issue. At the end of the day, we must remember work will always be there, and we alone need to manage our technology and its impact on our work-life balance. [244]

Mindfulness practices, such as meditation, yoga, and deep breathing exercises, can help individuals cope with the challenges of the digital age by promoting mental well-being, resilience, and self-awareness. Some key benefits of mindfulness practices include the following:

- Stress reduction: Mindfulness practices have been shown to reduce stress levels, leading to improved mental health and overall well-being. Ignoring or denying stress or even trying to distract ourselves may be effective in the short term but can actually undermine our health and happiness in the long run. *Present-moment awareness*, which is a key feature of mindfulness, involves monitoring and attending to the current experience rather than trying to predict future events or being stuck on past experiences or feelings. Being aware of and present in the current moment has been shown to increase stress resilience and effective coping. I believe a large part of stress reduction in the current digital age is simply letting go and taking time away from our screens. Our screens are required at times for keeping in connection with loved ones in different parts of the world, grocery shopping, note taking, capturing memories, and other useful things. On the flip side, though, clickbait news, aggressive social media threads, and the general doom and gloom that is only ever a few clicks away all compete for our attention, and this lends itself to taking time away from digital connectivity to lower our stress and just be happier in the current moment. Pairing present-moment awareness with other mindfulness strategies, such as not immediately reacting to situations, deep breathing, and showing care and compassion for yourself and others, all help in reducing stress—and you don't need a screen to complete or use any of these strategies. [245]

- Enhanced focus and concentration: Regular mindfulness practice can help individuals develop greater focus and concentration, enabling them to navigate the digital world more effectively. It has been shown that mindfulness activities can help us grow our neural networks. By growing our neural networks, we are essentially rewiring our brains to find new and better ways to handle tasks and cope with stress and emotions. Mindfulness activities help us direct our attention to where we want to focus instead of letting our brain control us. [246]

- Improved emotional intelligence: Mindfulness practices can help individuals develop greater self-awareness, empathy, and emotional regulation, fostering better interpersonal relationships and decision-making. Mindfulness can improve our communication and relationships as we become more present and attentive to our interactions with others. Listening actively and responding thoughtfully and empathetically are all components of emotional intelligence. As technology integrates into our lives, the need to consciously focus on building our EI becomes more critical. Soft skills will continue to become more important in this age of technology, where human connection and understanding each other and our differences will be increasingly valued. [247]

To maintain mental well-being in the digital age, individuals can adopt several strategies, such as the following:

- Setting boundaries: Establishing clear boundaries between work and personal life, as well as limiting exposure to digital devices and social media, can help individuals maintain a healthy balance and protect their mental well-being. The lack of physical boundaries between work and home means we must set other boundaries in order to preserve our time for home and work. These boundaries are built on habits such as not defaulting to checking emails simply because you can or because the TV show you're watching is on an ad break. Boundaries can also be in agreement with others so that you manage your time the way you intend to and not inadvertently at the whim of others. This could be agreeing with your partner who cooks dinner while the other catches up on work, or who spends time with the kids if the other parent has work to do. Even better, it could be agreeing to finish work on time two days a week to get out for a family walk to see the sunset. Your email inbox is just a convenient way for others to try to prioritise your time for you. Remember, you control the narrative. If other people are trying to contact you outside your work hours, it's on you whether you engage with it then and there or leave it till the following day. I have found a family calendar to be a great way of setting boundaries and have recently rediscovered the hobby of reading, which takes me away from my digital screens and social media for an evening. [248]

- Prioritising self-care: Engaging in regular self-care practices, such as exercise, proper nutrition, and sufficient sleep, can help individuals maintain their mental and physical health in the digital age. Set good routines and practice self-discipline. You won't always be motivated, so you will have to rely on discipline at times. Establish healthy sleep habits by creating tech-free times before bed. Blue light emission from our screens is known to affect the chemical balance in our brains as our bodies wind down for the night. Physical activity is also important, in any form of exercising that gets you moving, be it yoga, walking, running, or cycling. Whatever you enjoy and can or are willing to make time for not only improves your physical health but also positively impacts your mental health. Exploring offline hobbies, such as reading physical books, gardening, or building something, can provide a healthy alternative to your digital life. [249]

- Seeking social connections: Fostering strong social connections and engaging in meaningful face-to-face interactions can counteract feelings of isolation and loneliness that may arise from excessive digital engagement. The digital age has also contributed to an age of disconnection. Try to reserve digital communication tools like text messages, emails, and apps for low-bandwidth conversations. Favour in-person meetings or face-to-face catch-ups for in-depth conversations. When you are in the same room as people you are conversing with, you can read body language, facial expressions, and the general energy. [250]

Organisations and governments play a vital role in promoting mental well-being in a digital world by doing the following:

- Implementing mental health policies and programs: Organisations and governments should prioritise mental health by implementing policies and programs that support the well-being of individuals, such as mental health awareness initiatives, flexible work arrangements, and access to mental health resources. Governments and businesses should advocate for a whole-of-government and whole-of-society response built on a shared vision for the future of mental health across society. By implementing strategies to promote a healthy relationship with technology, we can start to normalise the topic and make it comfortable for people to talk about mental health and share experiences. If we remove the stigma from the topic, we can start to make true inroads into solving the mental health issues that have arisen due to a saturation of technology at home and in the workplace. [251]

- Encouraging mindfulness practices: Organisations and governments can promote mindfulness practices by offering resources, workshops, and training programs that encourage individuals to prioritise mental well-being. As our world continues to become more connected and online all the time, we need to commit funding to activities, strategies, workshops, and education on mental health. Host a breakfast or yoga class, start a run club, organise an outdoor event day—anything that takes people out of their work environment to engage with mental health and mindfulness. More often than not, we will find a lot of people struggling in this area who simply don't talk about it because they think no one else is going through hard times, or they fear speaking up and identifying themselves as not coping.

- Creating supportive environments: Organisations and governments should foster supportive environments that encourage open dialogue about mental health and well-being, helping to destigmatise mental health issues and ensure that individuals feel comfortable seeking support when needed. Employee access programs (EAPs) are great places to start. We need to continue promoting these services to our families and colleagues. Mental health is part of our overall well-being, but it simply doesn't attract the attention it deserves. Mental health includes emotional, psychological, and social well-being. This means it impacts multiple areas of our lives. It also impacts how we feel, think, act, and relate to others. [252]

In the labyrinth of the digital age, where the pace is relentless and the boundaries between reality and the virtual world blur, the sanctuary of mindfulness and mental well-being becomes an anchor for preserving our intrinsic humanity. As we reach the concluding notes of this chapter, the significance of these aspects becomes resoundingly clear.

Mindfulness, like a compass guiding us through the digital world of information overload and digital distractions, empowers us to be present in a world that constantly pulls us into the past or thrusts us into an uncertain future. This section's journey highlights mindfulness as a guidepost that allows us to find comfort amidst the chaos, to centre ourselves when the digital whirlwind threatens to invoke stress and anxiety.

Yet, the pursuit of mental well-being is not merely an individual endeavour; it is a collective responsibility that organisations and governments share. This section underscored the symbiotic relationship between individual well-being and the harmonious ecosystem of our workplaces and societies. It magnifies the role of organisations in fostering environments that prioritise mental health, and it underscores the imperative for governments to continue delivering policies that promote mental well-being, creating a foundation upon which individuals can thrive.

[242] https://slack.com/intl/en-au/blog/productivity/overcoming-information-overload-in-the-workplace

[243] https://www.theguardian.com/global/2021/aug/22/how-digital-media-turned-us-all-into-dopamine-addicts-and-what-we-can-do-to-break-the-cycle

[244] https://www.hcamag.com/ca/specialization/corporate-wellness/blurred-lines-the-dangers-of-work-life-imbalance/254466

[245] https://www.mindful.org/how-to-manage-stress-with-mindfulness-and-meditation/#mindfulness

[246] https://www.forbes.com/sites/lucianapaulise/2021/06/07/4-steps-to-improve-your-focus-with-mindfulness/?sh=3802dbfb34c1

[247] https://www.linkedin.com/pulse/connection-between-emotional-intelligence-mindfulness-andersyn-ph-d-/

[248] https://www.forbes.com/sites/carolinecenizalevine/2020/06/07/how-to-set-boundaries-between-work-and-home/?sh=41791d9e50e9

[249] https://www.linkedin.com/pulse/finding-balance-digital-age-prioritising-your-sukanta-banerjee/

[250] https://www.forbes.com/sites/rhettpower/2020/03/29/how-to-foster-a-culture-of-connection-in-the-digital-age/?sh=59220e1e50ca

[251] https://moderndiplomacy.eu/2023/06/14/mental-health-in-the-digital-age-navigating-the-impact-of-technology/

[252] https://info.totalwellnesshealth.com/blog/mental-health-awareness-month-activities-

Strategies for Managing Stress, Anxiety, and Digital Overload

In the throes of our modern, digitally driven existence, the harmony of mental well-being can often be disrupted by the dissonance of stress, anxiety, and the overwhelming tide of digital engagement. The essence of preserving our humanity lies not only in technological advancement but also in our ability to navigate these challenges with resilience and grace. This chapter will outline the path towards fostering mental equilibrium and safeguarding the delicate balance that defines us as human beings.

Stress can easily derail and disrupt the harmonious rhythm of our lives. In the following pages, we will explore a series of evidence-based strategies designed to identify, overcome, and manage stress. We will further explore mindfulness, inviting individuals to embrace the art of being present and develop self-awareness that tempers the rush of modern life and cultivates serenity in its wake.

The digital realm, though a source of boundless connectivity, can also create cacophonous discord within our minds. This chapter recognises this challenge and suggests setting harmonious boundaries with technology, creating moments of digital detox, and embracing nature as a counterbalance to digital noise. These strategies aim to harmonise the digital and analog worlds, nurturing mental well-being in the process.

This section's composition beckons individuals to share their mental health journey with loved ones and invites workplaces and communities to join in. The art of maintaining mental well-being is not confined to personal realms; it resonates through collective actions and shared conversations.

Intentionally disconnecting from digital devices and social media platforms can help individuals reduce stress and anxiety associated with digital overload. Some strategies for implementing a digital detox include the following:

- Scheduling designated screen-free time: Allocating specific periods during the day or week for unplugging from digital devices can help individuals recharge and maintain a healthy balance. Have you ever considered how much time you spend on screens? Whilst these devices are entertaining, the amount of time we spend on them can be a problem. In the last few years, tech companies rolled out digital well-being tools and apps to help us track our usage, including how many times we unlock our devices per day, which apps we engage with most, how much screen time we have accrued, and how many notifications we have received. There are numerous benefits to reducing your screen time, from improving your physical health to making social connections and boosting your mood. When you put your phone or device down, you can feel more accomplished, engage in the real world, and improve your well-being. [253]

- Creating tech-free zones: Designating certain spaces, such as the bedroom or dining room, as tech-free zones can encourage mindful, present interactions with others and promote better sleep. Tech-free zones can be physical spaces, designated areas, or specific periods where technology is intentionally set aside or restricted. These zones or times can allow individuals, colleagues, or families to disconnect and engage in activities that promote relaxation, creativity, mental restoration, or human connection. I have a mix of tech-free spaces, zones, and times I use in my daily life. At work, three lunch breaks per week are tech-free times where I read the paper, have lunch with colleagues, or go to the gym. At home, the bedroom is a tech-free zone. I don't take my phone in there, and it charges out in the living room overnight. My partner and I always ensure dinner time at our dining table is a tech-free space where we engage with each other and talk about our days, what's on for the weekend, or what's happening in each other's lives. Some Wi-Fi systems these days also include functions where you can pause Wi-Fi access across the entire house or block certain devices from even accessing the Wi-Fi connection for a set amount of time. These are all simply ways to disconnect briefly or for longer periods of time and engage with what's happening around you. [254]

- Limiting social media use: Setting boundaries for social media use, such as using app timers or disabling notifications, can help reduce the impact of digital overload on mental well-being. Social media has undoubtedly brought the world closer together, but we may be sacrificing our mental health and time, not to mention inflicting needless stress on ourselves. Social media is where people curate their best lives. It's not real. It's a rose-tinted view of the world. However, people see this and think they are falling behind or are failing because they don't have a nice car, a big house, and all the material things people on these apps supposedly have. This can cause us stress and mood swings, as it leads to negative social comparison. Limiting time on social media is easier than one might think. You could consider moving your apps off your home screen. Out of sight sometimes does equal out of mind. To go one step further, you could delete social media apps from your phone completely, or decide on a regular time to check them, maybe limiting yourself to an hour a day. You could use digital well-being tools to track your interactions with these apps, which can then tell you when you are likely to engage with them and build new healthier habits around these insights. We have twenty-four hours in a day, and I think we would all be quite shocked if we really examined our digital habits. Make time to devote to a hobby. Pick a screen-free hobby and invest in it. It could be something as simple as learning a musical instrument or starting an herb garden. Switch your phone off during these times so you can fully engage in your hobby. Some may scoff at the idea of turning their phone off. "How will I be contacted?" they may say, to which I would counter—you are turning it off for an hour or two here and there. Some of us grew up in a time before mobile phones, and the world didn't stop turning. You don't have to be contactable 24/7. This constant consumption is leading us into information overload and negative mental states. We aren't even paying attention to what we are consuming. We're just endlessly scrolling apps and sometimes getting into conversations that often devolve into digital slanging matches, which sap our energy. Social media gave everyone in the world a virtual soapbox to get up on and broadcast their opinion from. I believe this is pulling society apart. Everyone is yelling at everyone else on these platforms, and no one thinks they're wrong. Opinion has replaced fact. I've seen people get into arguments with people on the other side of the world about topics that barely warrant the effort. I've then seen how this affects their mood and the stress and anxiety it creates. [255]

Practicing mindfulness techniques can help individuals develop greater self-awareness, focus, and emotional regulation, which are essential for managing stress and anxiety in the digital age. Some mindfulness techniques include the following:

- Mindful breathing: Focusing on the breath can help individuals anchor their attention in the present moment, reducing stress and anxiety. When you are stressed, your breathing becomes short and shallow. You use your shoulders to move air in and out of your lungs instead of your diaphragm. You may even hold your breath, which increases your heart rate. In contrast, when you are calm, your breathing is slower and deeper. Your diaphragm flattens and pushes the muscles in the abdominal cavity, creating more space in your chest so your lungs can fill. The extra oxygen you are receiving gets into your bloodstream, keeping your heart rate low and constant. This type of breathing can lead to a state of deep relaxation. [256]
- Mindful walking: Engaging in a mindful walk, paying attention to each step and the surrounding environment, can help individuals connect with the present moment and reduce stress. The practice of mindful walking is the opportunity to give ourselves a bit of a break from the constant mental chatter. We actively try to be in the present moment with every step we take. Don't think about work, that colleague that has sent a frustrating email, what's for dinner, financial burdens, whatever the stress may be. Engage with your surroundings. Pay attention and hone your focus on the different sounds and smells, the activation of different muscles as you walk, the intricate detail and beauty of nature around you. Let your mind wander; this is normal. Focus on where you are, not what is waiting for you back in real or digital worlds. [257]

Effective time management and productivity strategies can help individuals manage digital overload and reduce stress and anxiety. Some useful strategies include the following:

- Prioritising tasks: Identifying the most critical tasks and focusing on completing them first can help individuals feel more in control and less overwhelmed. Prioritising is not just about getting tasks done. It's about identifying and focusing on the most important ones. Not all tasks are equal. Some have a higher impact on your goals, whilst others are less crucial. Identify and rank your tasks. Evaluate them based on their urgency. Tackle the largest tasks first to prevent from feeling overwhelmed towards the end of each day. My favourite strategy is to map tasks to your energy levels and deadlines. I know I'm most effective and focused in the mornings from 5:00 a.m. to around lunchtime, so I schedule my large tasks for this time. I'm more cognitively engaged, and my energy levels are at their highest. Find what works for you with trial and error. [258]
- Breaking tasks into smaller steps: Dividing larger tasks into smaller, more manageable steps can make them feel less daunting and promote a sense of accomplishment. Breaking large tasks down tends to stop us from procrastinating, wondering where to start, or just deferring tasks altogether. This method helps us easily identify what step we should take next, and it also gives us a laser focus on the tasks rather than vague overarching goals. To break tasks down into manageable parts, consider the following steps. Look at the big picture to understand what the end goal is. Examine parts of the task so you can figure out step by step how you will approach it. Think about the logical order tasks need to be completed in. Create a timeline so you can manage your time and effort. Finish the tasks with enough time left over that you can review your final output. [259]
- Using productivity tools: Utilizing productivity tools and apps, such as to-do lists, calendars, and time trackers, can help individuals stay organised and focused. Focus tools are resources that can be used to increase focus and productivity. They are often digital applications or online tools such as apps or browser extensions that block distracting websites, manage notifications, or provide background noise that can help with concentration. Focus tools can increase our capacity for deep work, attention, and concentration. By blocking distractions and creating a sense of urgency, focus tools can help minimise interruptions and increase output. Calendars are a good place to start. By using a calendar to manage your time, you can block out parts of your day for deep work. You can also share your calendar with your colleagues so they know when they can and can't schedule time with you. I often block out two hours a day for "focus time" and use that time based on what needs to be done. It may be deep work such as writing a business case or report that needs my undivided attention, or it may simply be replying to emails and catching up on general communications. My time outside of work is precious, so if I do need to do extra work, I set a timer, which helps drive a sense of urgency that I need to get done with what I set out to achieve in that time frame. Even the simple Do Not Disturb function on my phone

helps minimise distractions. I'm guilty of reaching for my phone and doing a little bit of mindless scrolling when I hit a roadblock on tasks, and setting my phone to Do Not Disturb means my notifications are muted and I don't have social media pings dragging me away from my work. [260]

Having a strong support system is vital for managing stress, anxiety, and digital overload. Some strategies for building a support system include the following:

- Connecting with friends and family: Engaging in regular communication and spending quality time with loved ones can help individuals feel supported and understood. Be open to communicating with your loved ones if you are feeling the stress or anxiety of life in today's ever-connected digital age. I've recently started sharing my feelings more with my wife when I am feeling the strain, and just talking about it helps release some of that self-imposed burden. It's hard, but if you can start to recognise the feelings of stress and anxiety appearing, you can catch yourself and take a breather. We all have people who care about us, so try to be open with them about your feelings. Don't feel like a burden; the truth is they will actually appreciate you speaking up about your feelings, and you may even find some common ground. You would be surprised just how many of us feel the pinch of digital overload. Talking about it is much better than burying your feelings and trying to overcome them yourself, leaving your family and loved ones wondering what may be wrong with you or why you are not yourself or upset and angry.
- Joining support groups or communities: Connecting with others who share similar experiences or challenges can provide a sense of belonging and help individuals cope with stress and anxiety. Internet and technology addiction groups are more common than you may think. Group support communities can offer online or face-to-face meetings to discuss and explore solutions to curb excessive technology use.
- Seeking professional help: If stress, anxiety, or digital overload becomes overwhelming, individuals should consider seeking support from mental health professionals, such as therapists or counsellors. Talking to professionals about your issues around technology and digital information overload can be helpful to help identify and break usage patterns you may not even recognise. A non-biased external party will be able to assist you in identifying the cause and solution to dealing with and even removing the stress and anxiety around the digital pervasion of our lives.

In summary the significance of managing stress, anxiety, and the overwhelming digital inundation in the era of AI resonates powerfully. It stands as a testament to our commitment to safeguarding the sanctity of our mental well-being and preserving the core of our humanity.

The digital age, brimming with its promises and conveniences, also ushers in a torrent of stressors and anxieties that can potentially erode our mental well-being. The chapter has underscored the imperative of addressing these challenges head-on, not as insurmountable obstacles but as opportunities to cultivate resilience, balance, and emotional equilibrium.

In response to this imperative, the chapter details an array of practical strategies akin to tools in a mental well-being toolkit. The digital detox, a modern sabbatical from the digital realm, emerges as a lifeline to regain perspective and break free from the incessant digital stream. It reflects the foresight of disconnecting to reconnect as we endeavour to strike a happy medium or balance between the virtual and the real.

Embracing mindfulness practices offers an approach for navigating the dissonance of information, guiding us to cultivate presence and self-awareness. It's a reminder to pause amidst the digital frenzy, breathe, and reconnect with our thoughts, emotions, and sensations in the moment. This chapter's journey emphasises mindfulness as the antidote to the rapid pace of the digital realm—a practice that rekindles our connection with the present, nurturing our mental equilibrium.

Time management, once viewed through the lens of digital demands, transforms into an important strategy to personally develop. Effective time allocation becomes an acute act of self-care, allowing us to create space for both digital engagement and rejuvenation. It's a testament to our ability to harness the digital surge without succumbing to its torrents, a skill that shields our mental well-being.

Building a support system stands as a specific remedy for the isolation that sometimes accompanies the digital age. This chapter narrated the value of connecting with others, seeking solace and guidance from our communities when digital overload threatens to engulf us. It's a portrayal of human resilience in the face of digital adversity, fostering connections that serve as pillars of strength.

In this chapter's conclusion, we emphasise the significance of these strategies as safeguards for our mental well-being. They are not just tactics; they demonstrate our natural ability to adapt, grow, and protect our humanity even amid technological changes. The chapter's culmination serves as a call to action, reminding us that by addressing stress, anxiety, and digital overload, we forge a path towards a future where our mental well-being flourishes, and our humanity prospers.

[253] https://www.mayoclinichealthsystem.org/hometown-health/featured-topic/5-ways-slimming-screen-time-is-good-for-your-health#:~:text=Children%20who%20spend%20more%20time,screen%20time%20can%20improve%20focus.

[254] https://medium.com/@mansinemiwal/5-steps-to-create-tech-free-zone-57b9ebc68c1c

[255] https://au.reachout.com/articles/5-ways-to-tame-your-social-media-use

[256] https://www.forbes.com/sites/bryanrobinson/2021/10/04/mindful-breathing-is-the-miracle-cure-when-career-stress-steals-your-breath-away/?sh=7ef6621966e4

[257] https://positivepsychology.com/mindful-walking/

[258] https://www.linkedin.com/pulse/power-prioritization-how-get-more-done-less-time-persona-training/

[259] https://news.uga.edu/break-large-tasks-down-into-smaller-more-manageable-pieces/

[260] https://fellow.app/blog/productivity/the-best-focus-tools-to-drive-productivity/#:~:text=Benefits%20of%20using%20focus%20tools,-Leveraging%20focus%20tools&text=By%20blocking%20distractions%20and%20creating,the%20organization%20time%20and%20money.

CHAPTER 10: BALANCING TECHNOLOGY AND NATURE

The Significance of Nature for Human Well-Being

In the unfolding narrative of AI and technology, where advancements are often lauded as the panacea for modern challenges, we must not overlook an integral part of our existence—our relationship with nature. This enduring connection, deeply rooted in our evolution, plays a critical role in preserving our humanity and nurturing our mental, emotional, and physical well-being. Amid the ceaseless chatter of digital notifications and AI-assisted lives, the call of nature offers a profound counterpoint. In this chapter, we delve into the imperative of maintaining this crucial connection with nature and propose strategies to harmonise our technologically enriched lives with the natural world.

Nature, in its myriad forms, has long provided the canvas for human existence. It influences our well-being, shapes cultures, and imbues our lives with fundamental joys. The rustle of leaves, the play of light on a woodland path, or the relentless rhythm of ocean waves evoke a sense of tranquillity, joy, and awe. Science, too, confirms the holistic benefits of nature engagement—reduced stress, improved mood, cognitive benefits, and even enhanced immunity are among the myriad benefits corroborated by research.

However, as we navigate through the age of AI, we often find ourselves entangled in the digital mesh, increasingly distanced from the natural world. This disconnection from nature, often referred to as "nature-deficit disorder", poses a significant challenge to our well-being and humanity. To thrive in the AI era, we must find ways to maintain our bond with nature even as we adopt and adapt to new technologies.

In this chapter, we'll unravel the significance of nature for human well-being, drawing upon scientific findings, philosophical insights, and cultural wisdom. We'll examine the profound impact nature can have on our psychological health, cognitive functioning, emotional stability, and physical well-being. We'll also discuss how a connection with nature can nurture qualities like empathy, creativity, and mindfulness—human attributes that shine brightly in the AI era.

Moving beyond the exploration of benefits, we will also present practical strategies to restore and reinforce your connection with nature. From green exercise and mindful nature walks to digital detoxes and biophilic design principles, we'll offer an array of approaches to help you weave threads of nature into the fabric of your daily life. We'll also consider how technology itself can support our connection with the natural world, suggesting tech-enabled paths to nature engagement.

Nature plays a vital role in promoting human well-being, offering numerous physical, mental, and emotional benefits. Some of these benefits include the following:

- Stress reduction: Spending time in nature has been shown to lower stress levels, reduce anxiety, and improve mood. Stress is relieved within minutes of exposure to nature as measured by muscle tension, blood pressure and brain activity. Time in nature significantly reduces cortisol, a stress hormone. Nature can also boost endorphin levels and dopamine production, which promotes happiness. Nature also has restorative properties increasing energy and improving feelings of vitality and focus. Being outside has also shown the ability to improve creative thinking. Something a lot of people picked up during the pandemic was walking meetings. I've tried this and felt benefits from putting the earphones in and taking a walk in the sun whilst attending meetings. I can take notes on my phone and feel more positive and engaged while I'm outside during some of my less important meetings. [261]

- Cognitive function: Exposure to natural environments can enhance cognitive function, promote creativity, and improve concentration. Time outside has been shown to improve memory formation and recall, specifically around short-term working memory and goal-oriented memory that requires focused effort. The theory is that natural environments contain "softly fascinating" stimuli that prime the brain for directed attention without bombarding it with distractions as urban environments do. [262]

- Physical health: Regular outdoor activities, such as walking, hiking, or gardening, can promote physical health by increasing physical activity levels and encouraging a healthier lifestyle. Because we are genetically programmed to find trees, plants, water, and other natural elements engrossing, being outdoors improves and promotes our physical health by reducing blood pressure, heart rate, muscle tension, and the production of stress hormones. Time spent outdoors in bright sunlight can increase our vitamin D levels and foster increased physical activity. [263]

The rapid advancement of technology and the pervasiveness of AI in our lives can sometimes create a disconnect between humans and the natural world. Excessive screen time, increased urbanisation, and a focus on digital connectivity may lead to a decrease in time spent outdoors and a weakened connection with nature, ultimately impacting our mental and emotional well-being.

To maintain our humanity and foster well-being in an AI-driven world, it is crucial to find a balance between technology and nature. Some strategies for achieving this balance include the following:

- Scheduling regular outdoor activities: Making time for outdoor activities, such as hiking, walking, or gardening, can help individuals reconnect with nature and promote mental, emotional, and physical well-being. Taking a step back is an easy way to fit in more time in the great outdoors and do something outside that you would usually do inside. Make time each day to go for a walk to the local park and read your book. Have your morning coffee outside on the deck or on a walk. Even mundane tasks like writing your weekly grocery list or replying to emails or texts can be done outside quite easily. For something more adventurous, research hiking trails near you. Governments and councils have invested heavily in green space close to metropolitan urban areas. Even here in Sydney, there are numerous hiking trails on the fringe of the harbour and city. Schedule time in your weekend for this. Because the benefits of being in nature are so profound, making time for the great outdoors in the evenings or on your weekends should be a priority. Just like you schedule time to catch up with friends or family and attend events or exercise, schedule time to be outside. [264]

- Practicing mindfulness in nature: Engaging in mindfulness practices, such as meditation or deep breathing, while outdoors can help individuals cultivate a deeper connection with nature and enhance the benefits of spending time outside. Studies have shown that engaging in mindfulness in natural settings does yield positive results. The experience of the natural environment is so fascinating to humans that it calls for soft attention, which allows us to disengage from our worries and stresses and pushes us to remain present in the moment rather than losing concentration or becoming emotionally overwhelmed. Mindfulness activities that took place outdoors tended to lead to better health outcomes than those that took place indoors. Researchers believe that this may be due to the fact that an outward focus may allow people to connect with nature more. I've experienced this several times when I've been on a walk during my lunch break. I will often end up on a little bush track that leads to a lookout point opposite the Sydney Opera House. Sitting there in the sun, focusing on my breathing, I have felt a sense of calm rush over me where everything leaves my mind, all the stress of day-to-day life just fades away. I would highly suggest that the next time you are out in nature you focus on your breathing, engage with your surroundings, and turn your phone off briefly. I do truly believe that everyone should try not only being outdoors more but engaging in mindfulness exercises whilst outdoors, as they can really have a positive effect on us mentally and physically. [265]

- Incorporating nature into daily life: Bringing elements of nature into one's living or working environment, such as houseplants, natural materials, or nature-inspired art, can help maintain a connection with nature even when indoors. In our day-to-day rush, it is easy to forget how disconnected we are from nature. Biophilic design is a research-backed approach to interior design that encourages us to connect with the outdoors indoors, by opting for houseplants or floral prints or simply using earth- or sea-inspired tones in our colour palette. These seemingly insignificant choices actually reflect the scientific theory behind biophilia, which proposes that humans have an innate desire to connect with nature. There is also plenty of reading out there on *attention restoration theory*, which is the concept that exposure to nature relieves mental fatigue. Indoor plants can boost your immune system, improve air quality, improve your mental health, and help with allergies. The use of natural colours, tones, and images throughout your home or office environment can have a soothing effect. Exposure to natural images pushes our brains into a more rested state. Likewise, natural scents and aromas can boost our mood and emotional well-being. Fresh flowers, essential oils, and even seashells or pinecones from your favourite beach or woodland can lighten up your work environment and make a positive impact. Biophilic design also looks at textures, fabrics, and materials of furnishings. People associate soft materials such as fur, velvet, and natural silk with happiness. So it may be time to upgrade your home interior or at least your study to use curved shapes that mimic nature and include natural finishes like wood, as biophilic design can make an impact on our immediate surroundings and help bring the outdoors in. [266]

Communities and governments play a vital role in fostering a connection between humans and nature by doing the following:

- Preserving green spaces: Ensuring the preservation and accessibility of parks, gardens, and other natural spaces can help individuals maintain a connection with nature in urban environments. As our cities move further toward apartment living over full-size home and land packages, it is more important than ever that local communities partner up with governments and councils to preserve and protect our green spaces and even deliver more of them to citizens. The urban island heat effect is where temperatures are one to three degrees warmer in large cities than rural areas due to buildings, roads, and other hard surfaces absorbing and storing more heat compared to surrounding areas. Green cover and spaces help to balance the temperature in cities and towns, thereby counteracting urban heat. Trees and other vegetation provide shade as well as cooling and cleaning the air via evapotranspiration. In large cities, the most affordable housing is often apartment living. There should be a focus on providing green spaces in and around these apartment buildings to connect residents to nature, green our urban concrete jungle, and make these places more inviting with a sense of community and wellness. [267]
- Encouraging outdoor activities and events: Organising community events, such as outdoor exercise classes, nature walks, or environmental education programs, can encourage individuals to spend more time outdoors and strengthen their connection with nature. The Outdoor Council of Australia (OCA) is a national body that advocates for and represents organisations and individuals that employ outdoor adventures and activities for the purpose of recreation, education, and tourism as well as personal and corporate development. Bodies such as OCA and even

state governments have frameworks in place to guide local and regional outdoor activity to encourage cross-agency and organisational collaboration to maximise the benefits of outdoor recreation for all citizens. Governments recognise the value of providing and promoting green spaces because it can drive personal development, foster resilience, improve health and well-being through social cohesion and inclusion, prevent healthcare costs, instil a connection with nature, and promote volunteering and tourism growth. [268]

- Implementing urban planning policies that prioritise green spaces: Governments can promote the integration of green spaces into urban planning by implementing policies that prioritise the creation and maintenance of natural environments in urban areas. Sydney, NSW, Australia, has the Public Open Space Strategy, which is a major step towards delivering more and better public open space that communities can access, use, enjoy, and belong to. It sets out a collaborative, coordinated, and evidence-based approach for governments and agencies to plan, invest in, and deliver public green spaces. It is great to see governments around the world finally understanding that public green spaces are the foundation for liveable communities. They understand people with access to space like this are happier and healthier than those without access. As development marches on due to population growth, rezoning, and other various factors, we need to hold our council and government offices to account and ensure they deliver spaces we the citizens can benefit from and enjoy being a part of. [269]

As we navigate the intricate relationship between technology and the natural world, it becomes increasingly evident that achieving equilibrium is pivotal for nurturing our humanity and cultivating holistic well-being. The juxtaposition of our technologically saturated lives with the tranquillity and vitality offered by nature calls for a harmonious integration. This chapter's narrative resonates with the profound significance of striking a balance between these seemingly divergent forces.

The age of artificial intelligence, with its relentless surge, has the potential to draw us further into the realm of screens and algorithms, inadvertently distancing us from the rejuvenating embrace of nature. The imperative, then, is to deliberately carve out moments for the outdoors, acknowledging the profound connection between our well-being and the natural world.

By dedicating time to immerse ourselves in nature's beauty, whether through leisurely walks, invigorating hikes, or simply taking in the soothing rhythms of the environment, we can rejuvenate our senses, rekindle our emotional resilience, and reconnect with the core of our humanity. These moments offer us a reprieve from the digital whirlwind, allowing us to recalibrate our thoughts, emotions, and even physiological responses.

Supporting policies that safeguard and conserve natural spaces becomes an act of collective responsibility. Governments play a pivotal role in preserving these sanctuaries, ensuring that our relationship with nature remains harmonious and that future generations can inherit the same solace and inspiration that nature offers today. By collaborating with environmental initiatives, advocating for green spaces, and endorsing sustainable practices, communities and governments can work in tandem to maintain the delicate equilibrium between digital and natural realms.

Ultimately, the chapter not only underlines the significance of harmonising technology and nature but also outlines actionable steps to ensure that we honour our humanity amidst the all-encompassing reach of AI. It fosters a narrative that reinforces the timeless combination between our digital achievements and the grounding essence of the natural world, inviting us to embrace the benefits that this delicate balance can bring to our mental, emotional, and physical well-being.

[261] https://www.ontarioparks.com/parksblog/mental-health-benefits-outdoors/#:~:text=Stress%20is%20relieved%20within%20minutes,dopamine%20production%2C%20which%20promotes%20happiness.

[262] https://www.takingcharge.csh.umn.edu/how-does-nature-impact-our-wellbeing#:~:text=Exposure%20to%20nature%20not%20only,the%20production%20of%20stress%20hormones.

[263] https://www.openspace.org/stories/health-benefits-nature#:~:text=Time%20spent%20outdoors%20in%20bright,will%20remain%20active%20into%20adolescence.

[264] https://www.reconnectwithnature.org/news-events/the-buzz/how-to-relax-in-nature/

[265] https://www.mindful.org/the-benefits-of-being-mindful-outdoors/

[266] https://www.washingtonpost.com/home/2023/06/02/how-to-outdoors-nature-home/

[267] https://www.climatechange.environment.nsw.gov.au/green-cover-and-open-spaces

[268] https://www.dlgsc.wa.gov.au/department/publications/publication/more-people-more-active-outdoors

[269] https://www.planning.nsw.gov.au/policy-and-legislation/open-space

Promoting Environmental Sustainability in the AI Era

As AI technology continues to advance and our planets health and sustainability continues to be a primary focus an imperative emerges—to innovate responsibly whilst taking care of our environment in order to foster a sustainable future. This chapter explores the pivotal role environmental sustainability plays in this narrative, underscoring the need to balance the burgeoning AI advancements with the delicate ecosystems that support us.

As AI shapes our future, it comes with a responsibility to navigate progress while prioritising ecological balance. This section delves into the environmental impact of AI innovations, emphasizing the need to guide these advancements toward not only technological growth but also the well-being of our planet.

The chapter underscores the need to bridge the gap between rapid technological advancement and environmental responsibility. It highlights innovative solutions that reduce carbon footprints, enhance energy efficiency, and address environmental challenges. These strategies blend technology with nature's wisdom, showcasing our ability to create solutions that benefit both people and the planet.

The chapter delves into the details of balancing AI with sustainability, from optimizing data centres to reducing electronic waste. It's a journey that reshapes our understanding of AI by weaving sustainability into its narrative, highlighting human creativity and our responsibility to the planet. It serves as a reminder that each algorithm, every line of code, and every innovation leaves an imprint on our world, and we are the ones creating this impact.

While AI has the potential to drive significant progress in various fields, it also presents environmental challenges that must be addressed. Some key considerations include the following:

- Energy consumption: AI technologies, particularly large-scale machine learning models, can consume significant amounts of energy during training and deployment, contributing to greenhouse gas emissions and climate change. To put this into perspective, according to TechTarget, the total consumption of one machine learning model over nine days was no less than 27,648 kilowatt hours. This number is more than the amount of energy that three households use in an entire year—and it took one program a little over a week to consume that much energy. Energy consumption has always been a concern with any new technology; however, the complexity of AI operations means it requires more energy than the computers and technology of previous times. To generate a life-like text response requires much more computational power and therefore energy than anything a computer could previously do. We also need to remain cognizant of the fact that there is a significant energy requirement that goes into producing the hardware necessary for AI to function. GPU chip manufacturing is at an all-time high as companies around the world race to develop and deploy AI functions and tools. [270]

- Electronic waste: Rapid advancements in technology can lead to increased e-waste as older devices are discarded and replaced with newer models. When old, outdated, or unused electronics get sent to the landfill for disposal, leakage of a wide range of compounds and elements occurs: lead, beryllium, and mercury, all of which pollute groundwater. This groundwater can be carried into nearby farmlands where the water is absorbed by crops, ingested by livestock, and can move up the food chain to humans. Unfortunately, once everyone has access to new technology, there is demand for even better technology, so we find ourselves in a self-made e-waste cycle. We now live in a society where life is as easy as it's ever been. We have promoted a replace not repair mentality. Why repair your phone when new devices are constantly hitting the market with better features? White goods, for example, can easily be recycled, such as kettles providing steel, refrigerators reused for their plastics, and so on. Mobile phones are more difficult to deal with, as gold extraction from these devices can be expensive and trying to recycle materials such as copper is unprofitable. However, we could shift mobile phone hardware design to a modular philosophy where units such as CPU, memory, and GPUs are replaceable, so when technological advances are made, old modules can be swapped out for newer modules, which could assist in keeping old hardware in service for longer. [271]
- Resource depletion: The production of digital devices and data centres requires vast amounts of natural resources, such as metals and minerals, which can contribute to environmental degradation and depletion. Life without technology is almost inconceivable, from mobile phones, laptops, and apps to cars, planes, and trains. These are all examples of how technology came to be an integral part of our lives. For all the benefits technology has delivered to society and the world, technology and the environment are intricately linked, and there is significant and potentially irreversible damage being done to our planet to deliver more technology to the world. The demand for innovation and bigger and better products all the time means mass production of devices never stops, which requires a vast amount of natural resources and raw materials. Many resources are being consumed faster than they can be replenished. Aquifer depletion, deforestation, fossil fuel, and soil erosion are all examples of how our environment is being affected as we try to quench our lust for the latest technology and gadgets. [272]

To ensure that the development and implementation of AI technologies align with the principles of environmental sustainability, it is crucial to adopt the following strategies:

- Green AI: Researchers and developers can prioritise the creation of energy-efficient AI models, focusing on reducing energy consumption and carbon emissions during the development and deployment of AI technologies. Some of those close to AI are beginning to question which uses of artificial intelligence are worth the cost of energy consumption and its carbon footprint and those that are not. Whilst AI can improve efficiency in numerous industries, does this efficiency cost more than what is being saved in labour costs, natural resource use (and lack of replenishment), and the waste that is generated? Many experts are now calling on the AI community to implement renewable energy sources into their operations. If the energy needs of AI can't be addressed practically today, the focus should instead be urgently placed on finding more sustainable methods of meeting the intense energy needs. We are at a crossroads. On one hand, As AI technology becomes more advanced, it will only require more computational power and hardware, which will consume more energy than it does today. On the other hand, if AI continues to advance as quickly as it has been, could it not become better and more efficient, allowing it to complete more complex tasks with less and less energy? [273]

- Circular economy principles: Embracing a circular economy approach, which prioritises the reuse, recycling, and repurposing of materials, can help mitigate the environmental impact of technology production and e-waste. As of 2019 there are now more digital devices on this planet than there are humans. In 2019 we purchased 1.52 billion cell phones, 785 million laptops, 128 million desktop computers, and 489 million Wi-Fi routers. These figures will grow exponentially over the coming years. A mobile phone is composed of over two hundred minerals, eighty chemical elements, and three hundred alloys and plastics. E-waste is one of the fastest-growing waste streams and is creating serious health impacts for our communities. We all need to start advocating for the "right to repair", as there is growing recognition that reusing our digital devices could be a way to save natural resources and address critical shortages. A circular economy recognises that we must design technology in ways that reduce environmental impacts, increase energy efficiency, and enable recycling and reuse. [274]

- Sustainable data centres: Designing and operating data centres with an emphasis on energy efficiency, renewable energy sources, and water conservation can reduce the environmental footprint of AI technologies. As newer processors are getting faster and hotter to deal with, the burgeoning demand of AI traditional air conditioning now found in data centres and offices will be unable to cool the next generation of servers. Will our data centres have to move to liquid cooling methods? Organisations must focus on designing technology that can deliver the best-performing cooling solutions in our data centres and offices for cooling servers, routers, and switches as well as other critical electronic platforms.

Governments, organisations, and individuals play a crucial role in promoting environmental sustainability in the AI era by doing the following:

- Implementing regulations and incentives: Governments can establish regulations and incentives to encourage the development and adoption of sustainable AI technologies, such as energy efficiency standards, carbon pricing, and research grants. Government policies play a pivotal role in driving the sustainable landscape of data centres and technology innovation. Frameworks and codes of conduct could help encourage technology makers to reduce their energy consumption through improved processes, energy-efficient hardware and software, and innovative cooling methods for data centres, manufacturing plants and offices. Incentives, tax breaks, and even grants could be offered to those that invest in energy efficient technologies or renewable energy sources. The benefits here are numerous. By reducing their energy consumption, companies can lower their operating costs, reduce their carbon footprint, and contribute to the global efforts to combat climate change, and if they adopt green technologies, they can create new jobs and stimulate economic growth in the clean energy sector. [275]
- Corporate social responsibility: Organisations can prioritise sustainability in their operations and AI development processes, adopting green AI practices and reducing their environmental footprint. CSR helps businesses adopt sustainable practices that have a positive impact on the environment. This includes reducing carbon emissions, promoting energy efficiency, and practicing sustainable sourcing and responsible supply chain management. Green AI involves designing and developing algorithms, models, and systems that are environmentally friendly and sustainable. The goal of green AI is to optimise energy efficiency, reduce greenhouse gas emissions, and promote sustainable practices. Companies that are developing their own AI platforms must be cognizant of the energy AI requires to be developed, trained, maintained, and deployed. Green AI is a good starting point to mitigate climate change and promote sustainability; however, it cannot solely replace policy intervention and individual or corporate actions entirely. We all have a role to play in CSR delivery. [276]
- Consumer choices and awareness: Individuals can contribute to environmental sustainability by making informed choices about their consumption of digital devices and services, as well as advocating for sustainable practices within their communities and workplaces. We all make choices every single day. What to eat, what to buy, when to recycle, and if we should walk, drive or take public transport. Whilst these can feel like highly individual choices, behavioural economics has shown that consumers are highly susceptible to environmental and social cues. This is why more needs to be done in the digital landscape to give consumers access to information and offer better insights into the environmental impact of our digital devices and the apps on them, their affordability and the availability of sustainable options. The relationship between our technology and sustainability isn't always clear or at the front of our mind when technology is so deeply ingrained in our day-to-day life. When you

are scrolling through your phone or exploring different apps, it doesn't exactly hit you that the app you're on is probably running through a cloud service and data centre, and you don't wonder how that data centre is powered, etc. The effects of your actions on your device are much further downstream. So first recognising that our devices do contribute to the climate crisis and then being more educated and making better decisions about what we buy and how we use our devices is at least a starting point. [277]

We urgently need to realise that the AI narrative and environmental sustainability are not divergent paths. Instead, they are interconnected, a manifestation of humanity's potential to innovate in a way that honours the earth's resources. It is a call to deploy AI innovations responsibly and with more thought to the affects this technology has on our environment. AI stands as one of the most transformative technologies with the potential to reshape entire industries. Simultaneously, the environmental crisis remains one of the most pressing challenges we confront. Recognising the profound interplay between these two forces and their substantial impact on each other should be a central focus in the years to come.

The chapter resounds with the theme of collaboration, where governments, organisations, and individuals unite in a common effort. It emphasises that each AI algorithm and every technological advancement carry the weight of a choice. Presenting an opportunity to move forward, to innovate and to realise our technological future but not forgetting that we have other challenges to solve such as the environmental crisis and that our challenges and opportunities are all closely linked to one another where actions in either of these areas is felt in the other both good and bad.

In conclusion, this chapter speaks to a collective mission—to build a future where the maturing of AI technology unfolds alongside the preservation of our planet's ecosystems. This is not just the story of AI; it's the narrative of our commitment to stewardship through actions and initiatives, and a testimony that our innovative strides need not be at the expense of our earth's legacy.

[270] https://www.spiceworks.com/tech/artificial-intelligence/guest-article/combatting-ai-energy-consumption-through-renewable-sources/#:~:text=Although%20energy%20consumption%20has%20always,ability%20to%20solve%20mathematical%20problems.

[271] https://www.electropages.com/blog/2021/08/technological-advance-challenges-the-e-waste-challenge

[272] https://www.ifourtechnolab.com/blog/18-ways-technology-is-harming-sustainability#:~:text=Resource%20depletion%20is%20a%20major,are%20all%20examples%20of%20this.

[273] https://www.spiceworks.com/tech/artificial-intelligence/guest-article/combatting-ai-energy-consumption-through-renewable-

sources/#:~:text=Although%20energy%20consumption%20has%20always,ability%20to%20solve%20mathematical%20problems.

[274] https://www.apc.org/en/publications/circular-guide

[275] https://ts2.space/en/sustainable-data-centers-the-role-of-government-policies-and-incentives/

[276] https://www.ecomena.org/everything-you-need-to-know-about-green-ai/

[277] https://www2.deloitte.com/uk/en/pages/consumer-business/articles/sustainable-consumer.html

CONCLUSION

The ongoing journey of remaining human in the age of AI is a profound exploration of how we, as a society and as individuals, navigate the ever-evolving landscape of artificial intelligence. It's a journey marked by both opportunities and challenges, and it's fundamentally about preserving the essence of what makes us uniquely human while embracing the transformative potential of AI.

As artificial intelligence becomes increasingly integrated into our lives, it brings with it a remarkable set of capabilities. AI systems can analyse vast datasets in seconds, automate repetitive tasks, create content such as text and images and even simulate human-like thinking and decision-making. These capabilities hold immense promise for improving efficiency, solving complex problems, and advancing numerous fields, from healthcare to finance to transportation and knowledge work in general.

However, with this promise comes a set of ethical, societal, and existential considerations. The rapid advancements in AI force us to reevaluate what it means to be human. How do we maintain our values, ethics, and individuality in a world where machines could mimic human behaviour and intelligence? How do we ensure that AI technologies align with our moral principles and contribute to a more humane, inclusive, and responsible society?

This journey necessitates a continuous commitment to several core principles. Most importantly is the preservation of our unique human qualities. Creativity, empathy, intuition, adaptability, and emotional intelligence are among the attributes that set us apart from machines. Cultivating these qualities, celebrating them, and harnessing their potential in an AI-driven world is central to our journey. Through these personal endeavours, each one of us can contribute to the creation of a society that not only values human uniqueness but also prioritises ethical considerations in the design, development, and deployment of AI.

Creativity, for example, drives innovation and artistic expression, while empathy fosters compassion and understanding among individuals and communities. Intuition allows us to make nuanced decisions beyond pure data analysis, and adaptability empowers us to thrive in an ever-changing world. These qualities are the fabric of our cultures, societies, and individual identities.

Additionally, the ongoing journey involves a strong emphasis on ethics and responsible AI development. As we integrate AI into various aspects of our lives, we must establish ethical guidelines, promote transparency and accountability, and ensure that AI respects human rights and values. This includes addressing issues like bias in algorithms and data privacy.

In parallel with individual actions, collective endeavours play a crucial role in inducing systemic changes that ensure the harmonious coexistence of humans and AI. Governments and organisations need to unite to formulate policies, guidelines, and initiatives that advocate ethical AI practices, promote environmental sustainability, and facilitate equitable access to the opportunities offered by AI. By nurturing a culture of collaboration, we can build a future where AI serves the common good, enriches the human experience, and mirrors our shared values and aspirations.

Crucially, the journey to coexist harmoniously with AI requires collaboration on the dynamic landscape of artificial intelligence's impact on employment and the workforce. We must examine the intricate interplay between AI's transformative capabilities, the evolving nature of job roles, and the need for upskilling and reskilling. This collaboration needs to address the potential challenges AI presents, such as job displacement, but also the opportunities it offers in terms of enhancing productivity and creating new jobs and professional pathways. Overall, the emphasis must be placed on the critical importance of adaptation, continuous learning, and strategic workforce development to navigate the shifting terrain of work in the age of AI.

The issue of AI and our environment centres on the imperative to align artificial intelligence's rapid advancements with ecological responsibility. We must start publicly talking about and highlighting the environmental impact of AI innovations, from the resources data centres and AI models require including how we can make these greener and more sustainable. All stakeholders, be it governments, organisations, or individuals, must embrace sustainable practices in AI development and implementation. This proactive approach underscores the vital need for circular economy principles, energy efficiency, and ecological stewardship. Ultimately, the significance of collectively safeguarding the health of our planet while harnessing the benefits of AI, encapsulates the synergy between technological innovation and environmental consciousness.

Ultimately, the odyssey of remaining human in the AI era is a shared responsibility that calls for continuous reflection, adaptation, and collaboration. It is not a solitary journey, but a collective endeavour, one that will determine the shape of our shared future. By willingly accepting this challenge together, we can design a future that not only revels in the unique qualities of humanity but also benefits from the boundless possibilities that AI technologies extend. This harmonious blend of technology and humanity holds the promise of a future where we thrive, not just survive, in the era of artificial intelligence.

About the author

Jeames Hanley is a Technology leader in the Architectural industry with over 15 years' experience in digital transformation and emerging technologies. Educating and training architects and designers on the benefits of digitising their day-to-day workflows and processes. He has spent the last 2 years deeply exploring numerous artificial intelligence platforms, building his own AI tools, and implementing them into architectural workflows as well as supporting the transformation of business support teams including people and culture, operations, and marketing through effective technology use.

Sharing a lot of his work on his blog https://www.aitecture.com.au/ and through LinkedIn https://www.linkedin.com/in/jeameshanley/ he is a recognised leader in AI implementation and digital transformation.

His career has included time working for architectural practices in the UK, New Zealand, and Australia where he currently resides with his wife Jasmine and daughter Maddison.